GRIN - Verlag für akademische Texte

Der GRIN Verlag mit Sitz in München hat sich seit der Gründung im Jahr 1998 auf die Veröffentlichung akademischer Texte spezialisiert.

Die Verlagswebseite www.grin.com ist für Studenten, Hochschullehrer und andere Akademiker die ideale Plattform, ihre Fachtexte, Studienarbeiten, Abschlussarbeiten oder Dissertationen einem breiten Publikum zu präsentieren.

D1720378

Pavel Girard

"The Fear System" - Triggering Tension in Survival Horror Videogames

GRIN Verlag

Bibliografische Information der Deutschen Nationalbibliothek: Die Deutsche Bibliothek verzeichnet diese Publikation in der Deutschen Nationalbibliografie; detaillierte bibliografische Daten sind im Internet über http://dnb.d-nb.de/ abrufbar.

1. Auflage 2011
Copyright © 2011 GRIN Verlag GmbH
http://www.grin.com
Druck und Bindung: Books on Demand GmbH, Norderstedt Germany
ISBN 978-3-640-99224-9

"The Fear System":

Triggering Tension in Survival Horror Videogames

Bachelor-Arbeit vorgelegt im Rahmen der

Bachelor-Prüfung für den 2-Fächer-Bachelor-Studiengang

im Teilstudiengang Anglistik

von Pavel Girard

Münster, 27.06.2011

Table of Contents

1 Introduction

Neuroscientist Joseph LeDoux states that

> [the fear system in the brain is] a system that detects danger and produces responses that maximize the probability of surviving a dangerous situation in the most beneficial way.
>
> (128)

LeDoux's definition of our brain's "fear system" serves as part of the following paper's title. This is due to the following reasons: First, it refers to the part of the human brain, where all our fears are processed, hence making it become both the ultimate destination for all external signals triggering fear (including horror media) and its place of origin. Second, it serves as an appropriate subordinate term for the holistic framework of techniques, which developers of so-called survival horror videogames[1] have established, in order to hopefully trigger "the oldest and strongest emotion of mankind", as gothic horror writer H.P. Lovecraft put it (qtd. in Perron, "Introduction" 3). Third, "surviving a dangerous situation", as the name of the genre itself already indicates, is the hallmark activity of every survival horror game[2], the latter being of primary interest on the following pages.

This paper aims at taking a close look at this "fear system", though, for the most part, not literally in the sense it is used by LeDoux: This paper does not take into account the neural processes working in the human brain, and it does not belong to the field of the neurosciences or similar disciplines. Instead, the techniques referred to by the term "fear system" and the relevant emotion tension[3], which is connected to it, will be analysed from a cultural/media studies perspective. In the course of this analysis, it will be argued that not only tension itself, but also several other emotions proclaimed as "negative" and provoked by

---

[1] Henceforth, the term "games" is used instead of "videogames" for practical reasons.

[2] As a matter of fact, in most action-oriented games, such as *Space Invaders* (Taito, 1978), "surviving" is the general aim, as Rouse states: "the player is thrown into a dangerous situation with a clear, undeniable 'kill to survive' (emphasis original) motivation" ("Match Made in Hell: The Inevitable Success of the Horror Genre in Video Games" 16). However, the constant threat of death (and the fear of dying going along with it) is much higher in a survival horror game, because the player is frequently confronted with depictions evoking tension and often particularly gruesome dying sequences: In the *Resident Evil* series, when the player is killed, the screen first turns black and then shows the character lying dead on the floor (*Resident Evil 1*) or being eaten or dismembered by the monster, that has killed it (*Resident Evil 2-3*). It is very unlikely that players of *Space Invaders* are actually afraid of dying, they would rather feel frustration than tension.

[3] The term tension, rather than fear or suspense, is used in this paper's title. It is generally preferred here, because fear, meaning "the feeling you have when you are frightened", is a quite abstract term, while "suspense" seems to be closer connected to the source of the feeling (the type of media e.g. games or films) than to the destination (the human body) of it. According to *Macmillan*, "tension" stands for "the nervous feeling that you have when you are reading or watching [or playing] something very exciting or frightening". Since this definition includes both the body as well as the source, it was considered more appropriate for this paper, where a game and the "bodily" emotion are explored in context.

playing a certain game can bring about tension, such as unsettlement, stress or disgust. It is assumed that these emotions evoke a basically negative mood in players so that they are more susceptible to be scared. This assumption draws on the film studies-related "Excitation Transfer Theory" developed by Dolf Zillmann in 1988, which Lee and Peng felt free to adopt on games (327-45). They state that "residual excitement from previous game playing may serve to intensify a later emotional state of a game player" (328). By arguing that feeling unsettled or experiencing frustration or disgust are in fact forms of excitement, Zillmann's theory can be related to the former argument.

In the main part (chapter 4), a glance will be taken at the "videoludic staging of fear" (Roux-Girard 145) of two different survival horror game series: *Resident Evil*[4] (Capcom, 1996-99[5]) and *Silent Hill* (Konami, 1999-2003). These specific series have been chosen, because, according to Picard (96), they are commonly said to be the most popular[6] and the most representative ones within their genre. The series will first be analyzed individually in seperate chapters (though frequently referenced to each other), and will later be compared as a whole in the final conclusion. In the end, it is hoped that the following questions will have been answered:

1. What techniques are used by game developers to trigger tension in the player?
2. How do these techniques differ?
3. Which of the techniques are the most effective ones?[7]

Hence several iterations[8] of the different series will be analysed, a close reading of an individual title (e.g. a step-by-step analysis as Carr did in "Textual Analysis, Digital Games, Zombies") is not possible, as this would clearly be beyond the scope of this paper. It is merely sought to identify as many "scare techniques" as possible in order to point out tendencies and pave the way for a more detailed analysis elsewhere.

---

[4] *Resident Evil* is the European title. The series is called *Biohazard* in Japan, the country where it is developed.

[5] The release dates of the games may vary, because most often, games are published in different countries at different times (a very common situation in the industry).

[6] According to Lange (15), e.g. *Silent Hill 1* and *Silent Hill 2* together sold 2.6 million copies worldwide, while the *Resident Evil* series (until 2005) sold 26 million (Pruett, "Resident Evil 4").

[7] Concerning the last question, it is rich in significance to note, that it is hardly possible to measure tension on some kind of a scale, at least not without conducting a thorough psychological study like Tamborini et al. did in 1990 (616-640). Since individuals feel and process tension (and emotions in general) differently, the intensity of a certain emotion, in all likelihood, depends on one's knowledge, viewing or playing experience and personal background, as suggested by Ekman and Lankoski (183). However, if certain "scare techniques" used in a game are labeled as "more" or "less" effective here, it is a mere assessment.

[8] Only the first three installments of each series will be taken into account (each as one body of work), since *Resident Evil 4* is technically not a survival horror game and *Silent Hill 4* is supposed to be not even scary anymore (Pruett, "Silent Hill 4").

Before broaching the games, an adequate theoretical foundation needs to be established (chapter 2-3). This is done by first providing a brief history of horror games, which approximately covers the time span from the early 1980s until today (chapter 2). The "general" horror game (in contrast to the "survival" horror game to be treated later) will also be looked into, because the latter is, without any doubt, a child of the former. Therefore, they are inseparably connected to one another. Chapter 3 points out the different academic approaches to game studies, specifically illustrating the dispute between the so-called narratologists and ludologists. The approach chosen for this paper follows this point. Afterwards it will be attempted to define the genre of survival horror after having shortly discussed the problems of defining genre in general. A piecemeal account deals with the psychological state of "immersion", which is argued to be a precondition for all videoludic emotions. The chapter ends with introducing some theories from media studies and psychology, which are drawn upon in order to help identifying some of the techniques triggering tension.

Current State of Research

Probably because of its "perceived low artistic value" (Kirkland, "Discursively Constructing the Art of *Silent Hill*", 314) and the often claimed "frivolous nature of video games" (Dymek 666), the academic field of game studies is still in its infancy (Bopp, Neitzel and Nohr, "Introduction" 7). According to Therrien (27), it approximately covers the last ten years. Thus it is not surprising that there are only a limited number of publications in comparison to long established "traditional" fields of study such as history or geography. As Bopp, Neitzel and Nohr have stated further (13), as well as Kringiel (16), research in the field is even more restricted, because it is still dominated by American and Scandinavian scholars. Furthermore, little attention has been given to the specific realm of horror games. As Perron has pointed out, only two publications have dealt with it ("Introduction" 4). Moreover, "consensus on what […] is scary in a game is hardly reached" (Roux-Girard 146), which provides convincing reasons for more research. However, apart from printed publications, several academic journals and essays on the topic can be found online within the framework of academic projects like *Eludamos* or *Game Studies*.

2 A Brief History of the Horror Videogame

2.1 The Origins of Videogame Horror

Games with a topic or setting which may be associated with the horror genre have already been developed within the very first years of games themselves (Rouse, "Match Made in Hell" 15): *Haunted House* (Atari, 1981), for example, featured ghosts, spiders and vampire bats. Nevertheless, it is debatable whether it may be referred to as a horror game, since the technological limitations of the old computer game systems made it difficult for their developers to create any tension, as Roux-Girard has pointed out (147). And since tension, by definition, constitutes the most vital element of horror (Carr, "Textual Analysis" 5), games like this may not belong to the genre at all or they do, but simply do not work along the same lines. However, it has been argued by Rouse that "the more realistic computer models become, the less capable they are of provoking emotions in players" ("Games on the Verge of a Nervous Breakdown: Emotional Content in Computer Games" 6). This, by implication, means that the less realistic graphics are, the more likely they cause emotions. But the graphics in *Haunted House* were so simple that one could hardly see the monsters in the game as anything else but "a white collection of pixels moving on the screen" (Therrien 30), and "the games' capacity to propose a horrifying experience", as Perron reveals, "obviously seemed negligible" ("Introduction" 5).

As soon as the hardware began to evolve and when it became technologically possible to depict more than elements "that sort of looked like a ghost" (Buecheler), developers picked up the typical imagery of horror, which, in most cases, was that of horror films. The graphics were presented in greater (and more gruesome) detail: The game adaptation of Sean Cunningham's 1980s slasher film *Friday the 13th* (Domark, 1985), just like the film it was based on, offered explicit gore within cutscenes[9], such as a machete vertically cutting through a human head. These frequently occuring scenes were accompanied by loud sounds that aimed at startling the player, which was, due to the lack of better hardware, a commonly used method[10].

---

[9] The cutscene is defined by Juul as a "cinematic, non-interactive part of a game, conveying the game's backstory or fiction [. . .]" ("Cut-Scene"). Though its degree of detail has increased with the evolution of the hardware, Juul's definition still applies to every game, no matter how the graphics look. Cutscenes can be "in-game" cutscenes (in survival horror these are often presented in the cinematic letterbox format), CGI cutscenes or implemented as films staging real actors.

[10] A further example of this can be found in *Rescue on Fractalus* (Atari/Lucasfilm Games, 1984). In the game, the player explores a deserted planet seen from a perspective simulating a cockpit, whose limited view alone managed to create a constant fear of the unseen. In one specific scene, the player spots a seemingly harmless pilot outside from a distance, who suddenly appears right before the virtual screen as a vicious alien. Its appearance is accompanied by a high-pitched siren-like sound burst (Ernst 24).

Surprisingly, the origins of "real" gaming horror lie in the adventure genre (Taylor 46; Wolfsteiner 157), or more specifically, in a most abstract form of the genre (Todd): Text adventures[11] like *The Lurking Horror* (Infocom, 1987), which, to Barraza, is "the great grand-daddy of gaming terror", were able to "generate some serious emotion and dread in the player". Playing, or more appropriately, "reading" the game, was perceived as something similar to reading a horror novel, "leaving so much for the players imagination" (Beech), and there is no limit to the human mind (in contrast to hardware). Although being a pure text adventure, *The Lurking Horror* also used music and sound effects similar to *Friday the 13th*. These had a particularly shocking effect, and created "a disturbing intrusion [. . .] accentuated by a sound burst" (Perron, "Sign of a Threat: The Effect of Warning Systems in Survival Horror Games").

2.2   The Evolution of Videogame Horror

In 1992, *Alone in the Dark* (Infogrames) was responsible for the first great revolution of the genre. The game introduced several features, among them the ability to move freely within a complete 3D surrounding and a fixed (virtual) camera, which displayed the game characters from different angles, thereby "fully embracing cinematic conventions" (Todd). The most important feature was the possibility of evading monsters instead of simply killing them[12]. The release of *Alone in the Dark* is regarded as having led to the birth of an utterly new horror game genre, "survival horror", as pointed out by Blum (26), Roux-Girard (148), Taylor (47) and Fesler (9). However, some authors, e.g. Schmidt and Ernst (81) as well as Kirkland ("Horror Video Games and the Uncanny" 1), credit *Sweet Home* (Capcom, 1989) with already having done the same three years before. In the game, several characters were locked in a mansion, forced to fight monsters in a confined space, with the "risk of permanent death" (Sterling).

---

[11] In these games, players had to type in commands like "pick up key" all by themselves, which made progress in the game difficult, since it often had to be guessed, which commands might work. In 1986, the adventure game *Maniac Mansion* (Lucasarts) introduced a more comfortable interface called *S.C.U.M.M.* ("Script Creation Utility For Maniac Mansion"), which made navigating through the game world much easier: Possible commands were depicted at the bottom of the screen, visible at any time, and were simply clicked instead of typed in.

[12] *Metal Gear* (Konami, 1987) did the same for the action game genre. It introduced passages, where the player was able to sneak upon the enemies, instead of fighting them, making it the first "stealth" game. In that pedigree group are e.g. the *Thief* (Eidos Interactive/Looking Glass Studios/Ion Storm, 1998-2004) and *Splinter Cell* (Ubisoft, 2002-10) series.

In the midst of the 1990s, horror games became even more cinematic with the boom of the obscure "FMV" ("Full Motion Video") games, consisting completely or partially of filmed or animated videos. *Roberta Williams' Phantasmagoria* (Sierra On-Line, 1996) is among the most popular of this type, owing its popularity mainly to its extremely brutal film sequences. Apart from that, it was a rather simple adventure game, players had to click their way through, waiting for horrible events to happen. Therefore, it "left no legacy to horror gaming" (Todd). Nevertheless, it is mentioned, because the genre it belongs to differs so much from other (horror) game genres.

1996 marked the release of Sony's game console "Playstation" and its first "killer application"[13], *Resident Evil*[14][15]. Both factors contributed to establishing and popularising the survival horror genre, whose groundwork was laid by *Sweet Home* and *Alone in the Dark*. With *Resident Evil 1*, Capcom adopted most of the features previously introduced by Infogrames (Schmidt and Ernst 78), such as the fixed camera perspective, the freedom of movement and the well-balanced mix of action and puzzle-solving. However, it replaced the complete 3D-animated environments with detailed pre-rendered backgrounds[16], which were made livelier by the use of animated real-time effects. These were integrated in the surroundings, e.g. in the form of water streaming out of fountains, fire burning in chimneys and the omnipresent blood splatters. Additionally, since these backgrounds were practically "photographies", the degree of realism was as high as never before: Whereas in *Alone in the Dark*, a ceiling still was nothing else but a green or brown surface, in *Resident Evil 1*, we could make out the grain of a table for the first time. The pre-rendered background visuals became a special characteristic of the survival horror genre and its popularity and frequency of occurence is mirrored by a plethora of good and bad *Resident Evil 1* clones appearing after 1996: part two of Capcom's in-house series *Dino Crisis* (2000), the first two *Parasite Eve* games (Square Soft, 1998-99), *Martian Gothic: Unification* (Take 2/Creative Reality, 2000), *Alone in the Dark: The New Nightmare* (Infogrames/Darkworks, 2001) as well as *Clock Tower 3* (Capcom, 2003) are only a few examles.

---

[13] This term denotes a nearly perfect game (in terms of playability, quality of graphics etc.), which is so successful that many players purchase a home console, just to be able to play it (Schmidt and Ernst 78).

[14] To this day, the *Resident Evil* series is composed of more than 16 games, mobile phone variants, such as *Resident Evil: Degeneration* (Capcom/Ideaworks 3D, 2008) not included. All games are more or less similar in their visuals, sound and gameplay. The fourth installment is an exception, because it was different in many aspects. For further reference see below (8).

[15] The first iteration of the series is originally called *Resident Evil*. However, to distinguish it from the whole series and to avoid confusion, it is referred to as *Resident Evil 1* in this paper (the same applies to *Silent Hill*). If a title is spelled without a number added, the whole series is meant. This is done, when certain characteristics do not only apply to a specific iteration, but rather to all games of the series.

[16] These are "static background images that are not drawn in real time [graphics]" (*Giantbomb*).

The latter game deserves more consideration, since it is characterised by an even stronger focus on evading rather than fighting: With the exception of the boss battles, in which the game character is temporarily armed with a bow, all gameplay relies on hiding from the enemies, who are constantly looking for the player. Therefore, it is not wrong to call such games[17] the most consequent form of survival horror. Because of this "flight factor", they are called "stalker simulations" by Weise (242), as derived from "stalker films" like Wes Craven's *Scream* series (1997-2011), in which "the killer is the main antagonist of the story" (243).

Silent Hill 1, just like *Resident Evil 1*, also used the technological capacities of the Playstation to create a new type of psychological horror. This was completely different from that of *The Lurking Horror*: Though still evoking an "imaginative and subtle anticipatory dread" (Perron, "Sign of a Threat"), *Silent Hill 1* was especially disturbing through its macabre game design, which featured humanlike, but disfigured monsters and rusty, decaying environments. The developers also wanted to show "classic American horror through a Japanese filter", as Picard quotes Akira Yamaoka, one of the creators of the series (114), staging the game in a typical American micropolis.

Further innovations brought *Eternal Darkness: Sanity's Requiem* (Nintendo/Silicon Kights) in 2002, also focusing on psychological horror, but evolving it. The game, which was obviously inspired by H. P. Lovecraft, achieved most of its horrific atmosphere by irritating and confusing the player: *Eternal Darkness* was "messing with our save games, controller and seemingly even our TV sets" (Barraza). The more the player encountered gruesome elements, the more visual and audio effects were triggered, including insects running over the screen, the shut-off of the TV's picture or sound or the apparent decapitation of the avatar[18] (with all effects shortly after being reversed). *Call of Cthulhu: Dark Corners of the Earth* (Bethesda Softworks/Headfirst Productions, 2005), a game adaptation of Lovecraft's short story *Shadow over Innsmouth*, was characterised by a similar approach: When being exposed to too much danger, "insanity effects" (Krzywinska 283), were triggered, leading to the game character losing its mind and even committing suicide.

---

[17] *Haunting Ground* (Capcom, 2005) is another example for a "stalker simulation".

[18] According to McMahan, as qtd. by Neitzel, avatars are "textual or graphic representations of users that include a character designed to fit into the fictional environment in question, complete with a set of personality traits, skills and health status" (196).

2.3   The Modern Videogame Horror

With *Resident Evil 4*, Capcom in 2005 was once more responsible for leading horror games into a new direction: The developers disposed of most of the genre's traditional features, like the fixed camera angles and stiff controls, and made the franchise overall more action-oriented. The virtual camera was placed directly behind the game character, in an over-the-shoulder view focusing on the weapon (resembling first-person shooters). Moreover, the general level of difficulty was lowered: Ammunition and health could be found more often and, for the first time, checkpoints appeared in a *Resident Evil* game. Tension relied rather on stress than on horror, by often confronting the player with a bulk of enemies at once. These "baying mobs" (Evans-Thirlwell) were agile and intelligent, contrasting the slow and stupid zombies of the previous games[19]. That is why many authors, e.g., Taylor (54), do not consider *Resident Evil 4* to belong to the survival horror genre anymore. Its successor *Resident Evil 5* (Capcom, 2009) followed the same recipe and, by introducing a cooperative mode[20], emphasised action even more strongly.

The horror game of today is exemplified best by the highly-praised[21] *Dead Space* series (EA/Visceral Games, 2008-11), which remains in the footsteps of *Resident Evil 4*, while staging its claustrophobical horror in an isolated space ship/space station scenario. The slow-paced survival horror seems to be moribund and has made way for fast-paced action horror, profiting from "the new generations of graphics technologies" enhancing "spectacular audio-visual effects" (King and Krzywinska 145). According to Beech, *Dead Space* "sits at the forefront of this evolution", featuring hordes of highly-detailed monsters, screaming at the player in Dolby Digital and state-of-the-art lighting effects. Its successor *Dead Space 2* impressed players even more through the addition of rambling explorations into outer space. These modern action horror games do a good job keeping the player in a constant state of "arousal", defined by Järvinen as "the stimulation of emotions as a result of fast action and high-quality graphics" (182), rather than focusing on subtle scares.

---

[19] The developers might have been inspired by the horror film *28 Days Later* (Danny Boyle, 2002). Here, the zombie-like creatures were also able to run and jump, never seen in a zombie film before.

[20] In coop, two players (or more) are able to play a game together, either via splitscreen or online.

[21] The *Metacritic* (an online database which averages out an overall rating of several critic and user ratings of specific films, games etc.) score of *Dead Space 2* was ninety (of one hundred).

3 Approaching the Field

3.1 Academic Approaches in Game Studies: Narratology vs. Ludology

To bring the academic approach attempted in this paper in line with the general discussion on horror games among academics, it is necessary to point out what these approaches look like. In brief, scholars interested in this highly-specialised field come from two different factions, the "ludologists" and the "narratologists", with the former clearly representing the bigger one (Eskelinen). On the one hand, narratologists (like Janet Murray) are open to theories and approaches from traditional literary and media studies in order to analyse games. Ludologists (like Espen Aarseth or Jesper Juul[22]), on the other hand, firmly reject such "limited" and "outdated" approaches (Eskelinen): They argue that games are completely new media which have nothing in common with traditional media forms like e.g. films. Thus, to them, "narratology is deemed less fruitful as an analytical tool" (Dymek 664) and, in consequence, games cannot be treated as such.

3.2 Linking Narratology and Ludology: The Approach of this Paper

However, games and films (or horror games and horror films) have a lot in common. Since the very beginning of the history of games, they have not only been thematically inspired by films, as in the case of the early game adaptations of popular films, they have also adopted many cinematic characteristics[23]. High-budget games (called "AAA"[24] games in the industry) like the *Call of Duty: Modern Warfare* series (Activision/Infinity Ward, 2009-11) employ the (simulated) camera work of a Hollywood blockbuster to evoke a clearly cinematic experience from a first-person point of view. But of paramount importance regarding this paper's topic is that especially survival horror games are said to have most in common with films. Two examples are the frequent use of a fixed camera perspective, which refers "directly to horror film conventions"[25] (Roux-Girard 151) and their "third-person shooter mode" (Pinchbeck 79). That is why different approaches, linked to different branches can be adapted to video games, if the aspect under observation finds its adequate partner in an academic field: The plot of a certain (story-driven) game, since it is a plot like any other, can indeed be explored with the

---

[22] All authors are held responsible for having written seminal works within the field of game studies. Murray's *Hamlet on the Holodeck: The Future of Narrative in Cyberspace* is a prime example for a narratologist's approach, while Juul (*Half-Real: Videogames between Real Rules and Fictional Worlds*) and Aarseth (*Cybertext: Perspectives on Ergodic Literature*) hold the ludologist view.

[23] Because of this, games in general and horror games in particular, are often criticised, e.g. by Rouse, who argues that in order "to evolve the horror game" one needs "to move it away from just emulating other media" ("Match Made in Hell" 16).

[24] These "AAA" titles, according to Dymek, have an average development budget of 5-10 million dollars (667).

[25] In the case of *Resident Evil*, it stems from zombie horror films (Lay 8).

help of traditional literary techniques to analyse narratives. Merely how it is told needs to be approached with the help of ludology. Further on, a game developer's methods to create tension are very similar to those used by the director of a horror film: Both make use of "startle effects"[26], for instance. The main difference is the important ludic factor of interactivity, which is, of course, restricted to games. Interactivity offers particular chances of scaring the player in ways films certainly do not. In that case, ludology is again required to fill the gap and cover up with approaches, traditional media studies cannot provide.

In this paper, games are approached in a similar way: Rather than strictly sticking to either ludology or narratology, this paper proposes an approach, which attempts to define a position between the two schools (i.e. ludology and narratology), as e.g. Roux-Girard and Ekman and Lankoski did. The following example of *Resident Evil 4*, though still favouring the narratologist's approach (in line with Zillmann's theory referred to earlier), pays its respect to ludology by embedding its key terminology (as provided by Järvinen [*Games Without Frontiers: Theories and Methods for Game Studies and Design*]) whenever possible.

Players have just fought their way through an enclosed zombie-infested area of the Spanish village providing the game's environment[27]. Because of the superior number of enemies and the enclosed environment, limiting space to evade the attacks, they have barely survived. They leave the area through a door after having achieved the contemporary game goal which was to solve a quick puzzle. Suddenly, they are confronted with a complete change in game tone: The enemy-infested, bright area has given way to a dark, gloomy forest with no sign of any monster. Still stressed and exhausted from the previous battle, the player is in a weak emotional state. While cautiously exploring the woods, all of a sudden a mutated dog with tentacles coming out of its mouth, appears and attacks the startled players. Adapting the example to Zillmann's "Excitation Transfer Theory", the "residual excitement" arises in the form of stress and exhaustion, which then intensify the "later emotional state", consisting of panic and shock. According to Zillmann, the former emotions would not be this intense, if there was not any "residual excitement".

---

[26] For further reference see below (16, 19, 27).

[27] "The space for play – boards, grids, mazes, levels, worlds" (Järvinen 338).

3.3 Defining the Survival Horror Videogame: An Attempt

Every cultural area has its genres and always, "the lingering problem of genre definition emerges" (Therrien 26). Sometimes defining a genre can be done more easily, as in the case of an "anime", by referring to an example from films: An "anime" is always a "type of Japanese animated film that often shows a lot of violence and sex" ("Anime"). In another context, however, producing a definition can be a complex endeavour, especially when it comes to subgenres: In the world of music culture, for example, no one really knows what the subgenre "Post-Rock" actually is (Schumacher and Steinbrink 122-23), but, nevertheless, it has been established as a proper genre. In this context, games are no exception, as we shall now see. Assigning them to specific genres poses even further problems, since the game industry is so much younger than e.g. the film industry. That is why there are no "official" definitions. However, scholars, journalists, game designers and aficionados alike have agreed on specific characteristics being attached to a game in order to categorise it as survival horror. A selection of quotations aims at delivering a proper definition of that term.

To begin with, in an issue of *Cahiers du Cinéma* it is stated that "Survival Horror - as the name implies, it's mainly about not dying" (qtd. in Therrien 34). Though this rough definition is certainly true, it applies to nearly every action-oriented game and needs to be extended. In the definition provided by Taylor, she not only mentions the theme of "surviving", but additionally brings up the obvious connection between that genre and that of "horror": "Survival Horror games earned their genre title because of their use of horror elements and because of their gameplay emphasis on surviving instead of thriving" (46). Elsewhere, Taylor quotes Richard Hand, who includes further gameplay elements in his definition:

> [Survival Horror is] generally understood to be a game in
> which the player leads an individual character through an
> uncanny and hostile environment where the odds are
> weighed heavily against the avatar.
> (48)

The gameplay elements mentioned are the "individual character" and its weakened position in the game ("the odds are weighed heavily against the avatar"). This vulnerability of the character, Hand mentions, seems to be an important factor in defining survival horror for many other authors: for Perron, it is caused by "not so powerful weapons and limited ammo and health" ("Introduction" 6), Niedenthal, quoting *Wikipedia*, concurs: "[. . .] the player is made to feel underpowered, generally fighting alone for the bulk of the game, with limited supplies" ("Patterns of Obscurity: Gothic Setting and Light in *Resident Evil 4* and *Silent Hill 2*" 170). The feeling of players being "underpowered", on the other hand, is not only the result of their "limited supplies". Weise, in addition, states that

> [. . .] the player must strategize, making effective use of their
> resources to survive [...] this is where much of the challenge
> comes from, since health-refilling items are scarce and enemies
> are numerous.
>
> (253-54)

The fact that players have limited access to ammunition and health is complemented by the fact that they are also outnumbered by the enemy ("enemies are numerous"). The same is mentioned by Kelman, as quoted by Kirkland: "the player usually takes the role of a normal human being in an environment overrun by demons, zombies, ghosts etc." (*"Resident Evil*'s Typewriter: Survival Horror and its Remediations" 115). To Lay, this is "quintessential survival horror" (37). Additionally, by the use of the word "normal", Kelman hints at the fact that the protagonists of survival horror games tend to be what Pruett calls "average Joe" characters ("Designing Characters to Be Scared For"), who contrast sharply with the highly-trained soldiers of most modern action games (like in, again, the *Call of Duty: Modern Warfare* games). Therrien also mentions this "ordinariness" (34). To sum up, all characteristics of survival horror having been pointed out so far (limited ressources, vulnerable and average characters and a superior number of enemies) serve the overall aim of the game developers, which is to make sure that the player is in a constant struggle of surviving. However, there is one last characteristic, which has the same function, as proved by Kirkland in a quotation from Egenfeldt-Nielsen, Smith and Tosca:

> [In survival horror,] the player controls a character who has to get out of
> some enclosed space [. . .] destroying horrific monsters along
> the way.
>
> ("Storytelling in Survival Horror Video Games" 62)

Nearly all survival horror games are set in a location, which is "enclosed" and thereby somehow isolated, e.g. the deserted mansions in *Resident Evil 1* and *Haunting Ground* and the barricaded, isolated villages in *Forbidden Siren* (Sony, 2003-08) and *Project Zero 2: Crimson Butterfly* (Tecmo, 2003). There is not a single survival horror game set in an open-world[28] environment as those of the *Grand Theft Auto* games (BMG/Rockstar Games, 1997-

---

[28] Open world games like *Grand Theft Auto*, *Saint's Row* (THQ/Volition, 2006) or *Just Cause* (Eidos Interactive/Avalanche Studios, 2006) feature a huge game world, which can be explored rather freely.

2010). Reasons for that are tension-related, and will be commented on later in the text[29]. Characteristics of the genre which have not been discussed so far, but are needed to arrive at a proper definition of survival horror, are a "fair component of puzzle solving" (Niedenthal, "Patterns of Obscurity" 170) and the perspective of the game, which is, in the typical survival horror game "viewed primarily from [a] third-person" point of view (McRoy), and is further limited through "the use of fixed cameras" (Pruett, "Designing Characters"). Against the background of those results, the following definition of a "survival horror" game appears to be appropriate:

> A survival horror game is a specific kind of third-person
> adventure horror game viewed from a fixed perspective,
> in which an often inferior protagonist, relying on
> a limited supply of ammunition and health,
> has to fight a superior and far larger number of monsters
> in an enclosed environment.

Some examples will now be given to unmistakably point out the difference between survival horror games and horror games in general, because "all survival horror games are horror games, but not all horror games are survival horror" (Weise 242). On the one hand, first-person horror shooters such as *Clive Barker's Jericho* (Codemasters/Mercury Steam, 2007) or *The Suffering: Ties That Bind*[30] (Midway/Surreal Software, 2005) provide an intense atmosphere, but because of an almost infinite ammunition supply, dying is nearly impossible[31]. The constant struggle for survival (or the constant exposure to the threat of death), one of the essential characteristics of survival horror games, is not part of the game. On the other hand, in the case of the first-person shooter series *F.E.A.R.* (Sierra/Warner Brothers Entertainment/Monolith, 2005-09), the difficulty is much higher than in the games mentioned above, and thus the player may die more easily[32]. Nevertheless, frequent checkpoints accompanied by an auto-save-function provide a quick reload, in case the avatar dies. These instances often make players restart the game at a certain point, probably just before they have lost their virtual life. Survival horror games, such as the *Resident Evil* or *Silent Hill* series, do not have checkpoints or an auto-save-feature. The player has virtually only one life (Fesler 8), and when this life is lost, the "Game Over" screen is the irreversible

---

[29] For further reference see below (18, 37).

[30] Though the game is also playable from a third-person perspective. The player is free to switch between the two at anytime.

[31] When playing on an average level of difficulty. In the case of a higher level of difficulty, dying is more likely.

[32] Though this always depends on the gaming skills of the player.

consequence. But more than this, the player can only save progress at very specific locations[33], which are scattered throughout the levels, often with huge spatial and temporal distances between them. Thus, it is not an atypical situation, when playing a survival horror game, that the player will suddenly die, will not have saved progress for a time and will be forced to play for half an hour to reach the "point of death" again.

3.4   Immersion: Connecting the Player and the Game

Before the player is actually able to feel a certain emotion triggered by a game, a specific "connection" between the player and the game needs to be established. Scholars have developed a complex range of suitable terms to describe this connection: "assimilation", "identification" and "mimicry" (Weise 241; Neitzel 204; Wiemer 180), "agency", "sympathy" and "empathy" (Ekman and Lankoski 188; Weise 241; Rouse, "Match Made in Hell" 20) are only a few of them. All have different functions, while they ultimately increase "immersion", the state of having "become attuned with the game" (Perron, "The Survival Horror: The Extended Body Genre" 137). According to Wolfsteiner (164), immersion is of utmost importance for an emotional experience of a game. The less we are aware of the "gaming situation", e.g. of the fact that we are actually holding a controller or staring at a screen, the more immersed we become[34]. A perfect state of immersion, i.e. the state of being totally unaware of the gaming situation, is called "immersive flow", "an almost-meditative state, in which you aren't just interacting with the computer, but melding with it" (Friedman qtd. in Neitzel 205). Different conditions enhance or block the immersive experience: Kirkland suggests "interfaceless control systems" being one factor making the "user no longer aware of confronting a medium" ("The Self-Reflexive Funhouse of Silent Hill" 405-06), whereas non-participatory cutscenes are said to "break into gameplay" (King and Krzywinska 148), blocking immersion. Wolfsteiner adds that especially fear itself makes it easier to let the player dive into the game world (161) and Perron suggests that particularly the horror genre evokes very strong emotions and therefore calls it a "body genre", referring to a theory developed by Williams ("Body Genre" 124). In conclusion, immersion may produce fear, while fear, at the same time, supports immersion as part of the gaming experience.

---

[33] These are typewriters in *Resident Evil* and note pads, glowing red squares and obscure signs in *Silent Hill*.

[34] Immersion is not restricted to playing games. We can be perfectly immersed by exposure to any other kind of medium, e.g. to a film or to a book. In a film theatre, the hall is not only darkened to improve the quality of the image on the screen, but also to make viewers become unaware of anything which might block total immersion.

3.5   Theories and the Method

With the help of the "Excitation Transfer Theory", it was found out earlier that several different emotions can create tension, which gives us reason to look at these emotions in the course of the analysis of the games in chapter 4. Another theory will now be used in order to underpin this assumption once again, and, as a byproduct, it provides an explanation, why fictional or "non-real" sources can elicit "real" emotions at all.

The "Two-Factor Theory of Emotion" was developed by Schachter and Singer in 1962. It is based on an experiment in which the relationship between emotions and physical reactions were explored (Pruett, "Ingredients of Horror: More about the Theory of Emotion"). The results, as summarised by Pruett, showed that "if your body feels excited and you don't know why, your brain can be tricked into believing that excitement is caused by some external stimulus" ("Ingredients of Horror: Two-Factor and Horror Game Design"). In horror games, excitement is different in nature and one of its forms is an elevated heart rate, resulting in stress. Pruett has applied this theory to horror games and has come to the conclusion that "physical stress, when combined with scary images, sound and backstory [. . .] is more likely to cause you to feel fear". Since stress leads to tension, as verified by the "Two-Factor Theory of Emotion", the "Excitation Transfer Theory" proves to be valid.

Finally, two popular theories from different fields are introduced, which will serve as vehicles for detecting some of the "scare techniques" in the games. To begin with, "Hitchcock's Bomb Theory" conceptualises a scenario of two people sitting at a table with an armed bomb placed under it. The theory states that if a spectator gets to know "that the bomb is going to explode at any minute, he will participate in the scene and feel suspense for the whole time preceding the explosion" (Perron, "Sign of a Threat"). The explosion itself rather surprises then (and this only for a short period of time), while the longer phase of tension before it is much more intense. Such "emotional alert" (3) is called "anticipatory fear" in psychology, which is also the core of the following theory, spawned by an experiment, conducted by Nomikos et. al in 1968 (3-4). It produced similar findings: Test persons were exposed to short film clips depicting wood mill accidents. The first clip showed a finger being cut off by a blade without warning, while the second showed the same, but was preceded by a sequence, showing the finger approaching the blade. The result was that the subjects watching the second clip were more disturbed due to "longer anticipation", whereas in the case of the first clip, they were less disturbed due to "shorter anticipation". According to both theories, tension increases, if the subject is forewarned. Furthermore, Perron (3) concluded that these theories are of help to differentiate between the terms/emotions tension and shock: tension results from both waiting for the bomb to explode and the finger to be sawn off, whereas shock is triggered by both the bomb actually exploding and the finger actually being sawn off. Applying this to games results in the observation that, if the player is made aware of a certain (possible) threat (e.g. darkness at the end of a corridor), more tension will be the result, in spite of the fact that nothing threatening has taken place yet. If something really happens, however, such as a monster jumping at the player from the darkness of the corridor, shock will be the result. That shock, as will become apparent, in survival horror games is mostly triggered by "startle effects".

The following method has been used in order to gather the relevant data: The games have been played (and completed) once by the writer of this paper. In the course of playing, the games were paused and notes were taken. The different techniques triggering tension were roughly assigned to the categories "visual/level design", "gameplay"[35], "audio", "narrative"[36] and "miscellaneous" and more carefully during the actual writing process. For reasons of space, several restrictions have been made: If two or more categories overlap, references to the other categories will be made in abbreviated form ("VIS", "GP", "AUD", "NARR" and "MISC"). A sudden attack of a monster, accompanied by a certain sound, for instance, falls both under the category "VIS" as well as "AUD". The same applies to the theories embedded: "HBT" stands for "Hitchcock's Bomb Theory", "AF" for the concept of "anticipatory fear" and "ETT" for "Excitation Transfer Theory". In the end, techniques (i.e. certain characteristics of the genre that serve tension), which have already been discussed in the genre definition, will only be referred to again, if they are deemed outstanding examples (such as the "weak characters" in *Silent Hill*, which are especially weak).

---

[35] Techniques related to the game mechanics are categorised here, such as "increasing enemy number".

[36] Techniques related to the narrative of a game are categorised here, such as those resulting in plot-related tension.

4 Analysis of *Resident Evil* and *Silent Hill*

4.1 Resident Evil

4.1.1 Visual/Level Design Techniques

"Environment" (> GP): A game's environment presents a proper departure point for the analysis, since it comprises most of its components[37] (such as avatars, monsters and the like). Niedenthal regards environments in *RE*[38] as "prototypical gothic" ("Patterns of Obscurity" 177), because much of its game design revolves around the concept of the "haunted house". This is notably evident in *RE1*, since it is primarily set in a deserted mansion. Looking at the entire series, environments are also stereotypical for the horror genre. They usually consist of laboratories (*RE1-3*), sewers (*RE2*), hospitals and cathedrals (*RE3*). They provide a setting evoking what Vidler calls the "architectural uncanny" (qtd. in Kirkland, "The Uncanny" 2) through "mazes of rooms and corridors [. . .] dead ends and locked doors", which "confuse and confound" the player (> "ETT"). Though players can choose between different paths, such as "go up the stairs" or "enter the dining room first" (*RE1*: main hall), the rule set[39] of the game allows little more than that: In general, players cannot escape through windows, unless the developers want them to, as in the case of the Raccoon[40] press building (*RE3*): Players have to choose between "jump out of the window" and "hide in the back" during the "Nemesis"[41] encounter (*Resident Evil 3*). "This maze-like linearity", as it is named by Kirkland, "produces a generic experience of tension and fright" ("Storytelling" 74).

Beyond that, every familiar and domestic environment is re-designed in an unfamiliar way, by removing almost all former occupants and replacing them with hostile creatures. This culminates in the apocalyptic setting of *RE2* and *RE3*, "Raccoon City", where all its "buildings are abandoned, fires run rampant and zombies litter the streets" (Weise 256), creating a mood of depression and hopelessness (> "ETT"). According to Weise (254), surroundings become even more "moody and atmospheric", when they are staged in a certain way, which brings us to the next point, the "fixed camera" perspective.

---

[37] "The resources for play; what is being moved or modified [. . .]" (Järvinen 338).

[38] For practical reasons, game titles will be abbreviated: *Resident Evil 1* becomes *RE1*, *Silent Hill 2 SH2* etc.

[39] "The procedures with which the game system constrains and moderates play" (Järvinen 338).

[40] For accuracy's sake, the misspelling in the original *RE* games has been sustained.

[41] A particularly strong enemy, encountered only in *RE3*. For further reference see below (24).

"Fixed camera": A fixed camera perspective, as stated before, is one of the main characteristics of the genre. In *RE*, the camera is not only used to create a certain eerie visual style, but also to decoy players into traps. Frequently, the camera is set in a position, hiding the monsters, as in the 2F east stairs (*RE1*): The camera focuses on the end of the hallway, which makes a sharp turn there. A zombie is located right behind the corner and since we cannot "see anything outside of the immediate playing screen" (Taylor 51), we do not recognise it until it is too late and we run right into its arms. The only way to prevent this is by slowly approaching the corner, which will trigger the zombie to move. Of course, there is no reason to act like this, at least not when one is playing the game for the first time. The limited view resulting from camera-control makes the player expect a threat behind every corner and thus creates a general sense of anticipatory fear.

"Evoking anticipatory fear (> GP, AUD)": After having played a game for several hours, players will become more and more familiar with its game mechanics[42]. They will learn, which creature poses which kind of threat and how they need to behave in order to survive. When they enter the large gallery in *RE1*, they will notice the bulk of crows, gathering on perches beneath the ceiling. Although these birds will be encountered for the first time, the player will be fully aware of the fact that no creature in the game can be regarded as friendly, but is rather to be looked at as a deadly menace. Both our theories (> "AF"/"HBT") can be applied to the example, since a certain effect solely depends on the outcome of the situation: The crows will remain on the perch and will not attack the player, if a puzzle[43] is solved in the correct way. That does not change the fact that the crows will be expected to attack (> "AF"). If a mistake is made, however, they will attack and the other theory applies: The players' awareness that the crows are dangerous and will eventually attack them generates tension, that is gradually higher than the tension felt in the course of the actual attack (> "HBT"). The boiler room offers another example. It is haunted by three "Cerberus" dogs, patrolling outside the fence. At a point, they jump over it and attack. The anticipatory fear results from the fact, that we can hear them running around for a time before they actually attack. The attack serves as a startle effect, which turns tension into shock.

---

[42] "What actions the players take as means to attain goals [such as to survive] when playing" (Järvinen 338).

[43] To gain access to a key item, players have to push the buttons under the paintings in the correct order.

"Startle effects" (> AUD, GP): *RE* is popular for its use of startle effects, also called "stingers" (Pinchbeck 83) or "jumps" (Lay 33). The example most often referred to by journalists (Schmidt and Ernst 78; Blum 26) as well as scholars (Perron, "Sign of a Threat"; Kirkland, "Storytelling" 69) is the "dog scene" at the beginning of *RE1*. In a narrow corridor, a "zombified" dog suddenly bursts through the window, immediately attacking the player. This attack is accompanied by driving music. "This technique", as Perron remarks, "is undoubtedly one of the basic techniques used to scare someone" ("Sign of a Threat"). There are scores of further examples, such as the following: in *RE1*, when re-entering the mansion after having completed the guardhouse level, nearly every zombie has been replaced by the more dangerous "Hunter" creature and on two occasions, they jump around a corner without any warning. While we are examining the keeper's diary in the employee room, a zombie breaks out of the wardrobe behind us. In *RE2*, zombie arms break through barricaded windows, reaching for the player, the floor of the library balcony collapses and a "Licker" breaks through the window of the storage room (B scenario[44]) and the interrogation room. Zombies smash a shed door from the inside and crawl out of wrecked cars, dogs jump out of fires and "Nemesis" pounds against the police station main entrance (*RE3*). Startle effects are particularly useful, when there are two of them in a row, as in the press building mentioned above (17): In a burning stairway, fire first causes a door window to burst, only to let the whole door be blown inside afterwards. Preceding startle effects with a "false alert" is also common: In the underground morgue of *RE2*, an unsettling place in itself, one of the hatches drops, but nothing comes out (> "AF"). Shortly after, another one does the same, this time releasing a zombie. The zombie itself also proves to be essential for the horrific experience of *RE*, since "the figure of the monster is at the core of the videoludic experience of fright", as Perron reveals ("Body Genre" 126).

"Creature design" (> GP, AUD): The typical monster in *RE* is the zombie. According to Perron, it is "abject and reminds the still-living of the inescapable decrepitude of their own material parts" ("Body Genre" 128), in other words, their mortality. It is an ambivalent creature then, eliciting both disgust and pity[45]. While disgust stems from its hideous appearance, pity is reflected by its constant moaning and its combat tactics: When being shot

---

[44] *RE2* is divided into four scenarios, two "A" and two "B". Each pair features a different protagonist, either Leon S. Kennedy or Claire Redfield. The longer "A" scenarios represent the main game, whereas the shorter "B" scenarios offer an alternative play from the perspective of the other character. Occasionally, the protagonists meet, intertwining the narratives of both scenarios.

[45] This is particularly apparent in case of the naked zombies in the laboratory levels (*RE1/RE3*), which seem even more abject.

(or stabbed[46]), zombies often fall to the ground to remain in a state of unconsciousness rather than death, which leads players to assume them dead. When they progress, the zombies suddenly grab their feet and bite them[47]. We fear most of the other creatures, like the mutated dogs (*RE1-RE3*), plants (*RE2*) or hunters (*RE1/RE3*[48]) not because of their appearance, but their capabilities: They are simply harder to beat than the rather weak zombie. Some combine both characteristics, however, like *RE2*'s "Lickers", which are naked and blind creatures with a long tongue and claws, capable of decapitating their victims within seconds. They can also walk on the ceiling (as the hairy insectoid lab monsters [*RE1*] and drain demons [*RE3*] can), providing them with more flexibility in attacking us. Other monsters are more threatening, because they are simply bigger: giant boss creatures like the mutated snake and plant (*RE1*), the alligator (*RE2*), the "Gravedigger" and Type III[49]Nemesis (*RE3*) are all "designed to make even the macho STARS[50] mercenaries look overwhelmed" (Pruett, "Designing Characters"). Finally, traditional imagery, having proven effective in horror media since those were created, is also mirrored by *RE*'s creature design at times: hairy spiders roam hallways, bars (*RE1*), sewers (*RE2*) and balconies (*RE3*) and an even bigger one can be found in the underground level (*RE1*). These will trigger disgust[51], which is unlikely to decrease, when they are killed and hundreds of smaller spiders crawl from the corpse (> "ETT").

"Door sequences": Rouse argues in King and Krzywinska (148) that it is "a strange concept [. . .] to disrupt interactive experiences with a non-interactive one". These non-interactive elements, of which the in-game cutscene is the most popular one, are often said to obstruct the immersive flow, as Rouse claims elsewhere. To him, they are "[. . .] surely one of the most jarring immersion breakers in a games toolbox" ("Match Made In Hell" 23). A non-interactive element in *RE* are the door sequences, originally created to conceal the identity of the loading screen, which appears between different areas of the game[52]. They show the

---

[46] The knife is provided as an emergency weapon in every *RE* game in case ammunition runs out. Using it is risky though, since monsters do not take much damage and the player needs to let them come dangerously close.

[47] There is a way to identify an "unconscious" zombie though: whereas dead zombies are surrounded by a pool of blood, this lacks in the case of the unconscious one. Within moments of heightened action, however (e.g. when more than one zombie is involved), this can be overlooked easily.

[48] The *RE3* version is called "Hunter Gamma" and is, as always, more dangerous than the previous one.

[49] Nemesis gradually changes its form during the game.

[50] "S.T.A.R.S." stands for "Special Tactics And Rescue Service". "S.T.A.R.S" is the special forces unit investigating the horrible events in *RE1-3*.

[51] In a study at Würzburg University, test persons were confronted with pictures of different poisonous animals, including spiders, which they "specified [. . .] as most dangerous and disgusting" (Bustami).

[52] *RE*'s door sequences have become a trademark of the series. For this reason, they were kept in later games, although they were not necessary anymore due to more advanced hardware. Apart from doors, the sequences also show ladders, stairs, elevators and vents.

animation of an opening door, framed by a black screen. However, the sequences have been programmed in such a way, that they simulate the player actually entering the room, shown from a first-person perspective. Due to the blackness of the screen, the player gets the feeling of walking into the darkness and the unkown (> "AF"). Moreover, due to the fact that the player is not in control anymore, the sequences "generate a sense of helplessness, heightened anxiety", as Ekman and Lankoski argue (196).

"Blood and gore": Since *RE* is heavily inspired by classic zombie splatter films like *Dawn of the Dead* (George A. Romero, 1978), gore effects are an important aspect of the series. Blood splatters like fountains when players shoot monsters or are bitten by them, zombies' heads are squashed, shot and kicked off. Even the players' heads are not safe and might be sliced off by the vicious "Hunter" and "Licker" creatures, low health provided. The introduction of *RE1*'s "Director's Cut" (1997), consisting of real film footage, shows a half-eaten human face and a disembodied arm, while the first zombie in the game is introduced by a CGI ("Computer-Generated Imagery") cutscene. It shows a zombie eating and a human head falling to the ground in the process, "ensuring that the gamer immediately grasps and feels the horror that he is about to meet head-on" (Perron, "Body Genre" 127) (> "AF"). *RE2* goes even further and shows human corpses being entirely ripped apart: a journalist's torso is split up by a parasite from the inside, the police chief suffers the same fate. Disgust is the emotion most likely connected to gore, though again, it must be remarked that feeling it is highly subjective. Scholars refer to a "morbid curiosity" (Weise 261), a "desire to watch" (Tamborini et al. 616), which Walz regards of dating from antiquity[53] (146-47). Thus, players might even feel a sort of joy, when they are being confronted with gore, while others might be repelled. According to Kirkland, this "compulsion/repulsion" relationship is in "the nature of horror videogame play" ("Maternal Engulfment in Horror Videogames" 2).

"Undermining players' expectations" (> GP): *RE2* contains a scene, which is unique in the series. Typically, when a player attempts to enter a certain room, the door sequence is triggered. Since this happens all the time and is part of the game's rule set, the player has most likely become completely accustomed to it. Once, however, in the outside shed, the door sequence is interrupted by two zombies, suddenly walking through the door within the animation. After that, they enter the "real" game space and pose a threat. Pinchbeck calls this "split between what should normally occur and what is to be specifically expected" a "hugely

---

[53] According to Walz, this "violence for fun" has its origins in the public lynchings of ancient *spectaculi* (e.g. gladiator fights). Though many people barbarously killed each other in the course of those events, the audience acclaimed nonetheless.

beneficial underlying feature" (92). Further examples are false alerts, which necessitate game conventions to be broken (and thus also subvert expectations): Both the mansion and guardhouse levels (*RE1*) contain bath tubs filled with muddy, opaque water and it is expected that something comes out or grabs us, while we are trying to pull the plug (> "AF"). But, indeed, nothing happens at all. This unpredictability is of utmost importance when it comes to horror, and in the world of *RE* is best exemplified by startle effects, discussed previously (19).

"Cutscenes": In-game cutscenes are mainly used to drive the plot forward, whereas most of the CGI cutscenes have the principal purpose of creating tension: When players have left the guardhouse level and have entered the mansion again (*RE1*), a CGI cutscene shows something, running along exactly the same route the player passed seconds ago and finally opening the door. This is seen through the eyes of that creature, which turns out to be a "Hunter" (encountered here for the first time). During that sequence, however, players do not know, what is to be expected (> "AF") and the speed of the unknown creature moving and the fact that everything is seen through its eyes increases the effect[54]. The first "Licker" encounter in the police station (*RE2*) is also announced by such a cutscene. Others rather provide startle effects than anticipatory fear: An attempt to open the door in the mansion's main hall (*RE1*) shows a "Cerberus" dog biting our hand.

4.1.2 Gameplay Techniques

"Increasing enemy number" (> VIS, AUD): A safe way to create stress is to make a game more difficult, which is achieved in numerous ways[55] e.g. by increasing the number of enemies. This has been done with every new part of the series. In *RE1* not more than three zombies could be found in a single area, while *RE2* already starts with a sequence of street sections, which are crowded by numerous zombies. Players need to navigate carefully through them until they finally reach the safe place of the gun shop. "Running the gauntlet" like this is likely to evoke considerable stress, which, according to our theory, usually results in increased tension[56] (> "ETT").

---

[54] A similar cutscene is shown in the flooded basement of the guardhouse, where a shark attack is shown through the eyes of the enemy.

[55] E.g. by making enemies more dangerous, reducing health and ammunition supplies or by designing complex puzzles.

[56] Though developers have to be careful that they provoke stress rather than frustration, since frustration is said to break immersion (Rouse, "Match Made in Hell" 22).

"Implying urgency" (> AUD): At the end of all *RE* games, the player needs to leave the area, which is typically a secret underground laboratory, before some kind of explosion will be taking place[57]. These sequences are accompanied by an alert, consisting of a certain "alarm sound" and a voice from a loudspeaker repeatedly urging evacuation. Additionally, several monsters (which have been previously defeated) reappear in higher numbers during this escape phase. Stress or even panic is the result and "when panic sets in, control is diminished – our performance impaired", as Krzywinska argues (285). This makes the player more vulnerable for the boss fights, that immediately follow such events (> "ETT"). In the course of the boss fights, a time limit is displayed, which additionally visualises the time pressure, which was only implied beforehand, thus increasing the effect.

"Traps" (> VIS): Most of the time, players can avoid death by playing carefully and using health items frequently. Sometimes, however, *RE1* introduces traps, which can kill them immediately, regardless of their health status. Five times, players are lured into such a trap: The ceiling of a room lowers, threatening to crush the players, rooms are filled with toxic gas and boulders run them over. Some traps can be avoided simply by reacting quickly (i.e. dodging the boulders and leaving the trap room through the other door), while others require puzzle-solving[58]. Traps are confined to *RE1*, though comparable situations of "sudden danger" can be found in the other parts, such as in the electricity plant (*RE3*): While the player tries to open a shutter, which leads to a key item, an in-game cutscene shows various zombies infiltrate the area, which also need to be defeated by solving a puzzle[59]. Such situations, in which players are trapped somewhere and need to defend themselves against invading enemies belong to the "shrinking fortress" phenomena (Weise 253). They also stem from classic zombie films.

"Invulnerable enemies": *RE2* features a special kind of enemy, which cannot be defeated until the very end of the game, where it appears again as the final boss. This enemy (called "Tyrant 103") is dropped from a helicopter and, from that point on, awaits the player in certain rooms and hallways. Tyrant 103 is much stronger than any other enemy and the player can either attack or evade him. If players choose to attack (and succeed), they are rewarded with special weapon parts and health items, making winning the game much easier. Regardless which option the player chooses, both are equally dangerous: a battle is difficult and during evasion,

---

[57] These are the result of self-destruct sequences in *RE1* and *RE2*. In *RE3*, the city is about to become extinguished in order to to keep the zombie virus at bay.

[58] The gas traps in the armor (mansion level) and operating room (laboratory level) are disabled by sealing the air outlet with a statue or crate.

[59] Players choose "Increase electricity output" (*Resident Evil 3*) to kill all zombies at once.

players will be hit at least once, since these encounters mostly take place in narrow hallways. A similar enemy, called "Nemesis" is introduced in *RE3*. Players are confronted with this monster early in the game and can again choose between evasion and attack. Nemesis is even stronger and more menacing, since he is able to follow the player through doors which no other monster in the game can. By introducing an invulnerable enemy, whose appearance is utterly unpredictable at that, the developers dispose of the reassuring feeling of "the shotgun to head satisfaction" (Lay 28) which a zombie encounter offers, leaving the player anxious and desperate instead and in a state of anticipating fear (> "ETT"/"AF").

4.1.3 Audio Techniques

"General sound and music score": Rooke[60] argues that sound is one of the most important elements of horror games (qtd. in Klatt, "Im Herzen der Finsternis" 72). The reason for that is that sound not only intensifies immersion (Walz 154), but also compensates for the lack of other senses, games cannot appeal to, such as the sense of smell (Ekman and Lankoski 191). As in many modern games, the sound of *RE* consists of both sound effects and music score. The sound effects (gun shots, footsteps etc.) are always identical to their real counterparts and therefore sound exactly as we expect them to. Since these real-recorded sound effects make the game more authentic, it may serve the purpose of immersion Walz is referring to. Not so abstract are the "acousmatic" off-screen sounds, meaning a "sound one hears without seeing its originating cause" (Chion qtd. in Roux-Girard 152). These can be heard in many of the outside areas: dogs are howling in the courtyard (*RE1*), zombies are shuffling around downtown (*RE3*) and crows are cawing in the police station backyard (*RE2*). They also "induce fear because they create anticipation" (152) (> "AF").

As far as music is concerned, it is difficult to describe how and why it contributes to the atmosphere of the game, without playing it. Suffice to say that the string and piano driven music is clearly inspired by horror films and always "reinforces the onscreen action" (Whalen): In the main hall of the mansion (*RE1*) and the police station (*RE2*), music is dramatic and opulent and an echoing effect is included to emphasise the vastness of the architecture. In the guard house (*RE1*), however, which consists of rather narrow corridors, the "tinkling" score contributes to the claustrophobic effect (> "ETT").

---

[60] Frank Rooke is a game developer and his studio Monolith are responsible for several horror games like the *Blood* (GT Interactive, 1997-98), *F.E.A.R.* and *Condemned* (Sega, 2005-08) series.

4.1.4 Narrative Techniques

"Remediation": Including "old" media in a certain game is termed "remediation" by Kirkland ("Self-Reflexive Funhouse" 408). In survival horror games, remediation frequently appears in the form of TV sets, radios, photos, celluloid films or slides. Notes (like e.g. diaries) are a further type of remediation, scattered throughout the game world. They are used to create an uncanny atmosphere through their horrific content. Particularly in *RE*, this content is often of macabre and gory nature, as exemplified by a diary, which can be found in the employee room (*RE1*):

> One of the higher-ups assigned me to take care of a new creature.
> It looks like a skinned gorilla [. . .] When I threw in a pig, the creature
> seemed to play with it... tearing off the pig's legs and pulling out
> the guts before it actually started eating.
> (*Resident Evil*)

The last entry of the same diary is "Itchy. Tasty.", implying that the keeper has ultimately turned into a zombie, which is confirmed shortly after[61]. That "turns a simple note into an indicator of threat" (McCrea 222) (> "AF"). Besides that, notes have a narrative function, driving the plot forward. This not only contributes to the general plot related tension ("How did everyone become zombified?" Kirkland, "Storytelling" 75), but also to "a sense of the real", as Kirkland suggests elsewhere ("*Resident Evil*'s Typewriter: Survival Horror and its Remediations" 115), serving, at the same time, the purpose of immersion.

4.1.5 Miscellaneous Techniques

"Vibration": Controller vibration accompanies most of the action events in *RE* and differs in its frequence and duration: single impulses accompany startle effects and enemy attacks, a row of short impulses is used to simulate heart beat. Earthquakes and explosions (*RE3*) result in longer vibration. This not only "increases tension during gameplay" (Taylor 52), it also synchronises avatar, interface (controller) and the player, thus producing deeper immersion.

---

[61] For further reference see above (19).

4.2 Silent Hill

4.2.1 Visual/Level Design Techniques

"Environment" (> NARR, AUD): At first sight, the environment is similar to that of *RE*, drawing on the same horror film clichés: A deserted midwestern town, filled with its typical buildings (schools, hospitals etc.). However, the concept of the unfamiliar invading the familiar[62] proves to be very different in *SH*. It is embodied by the "Otherworld", a sort of parallel universe, the protagonists are (involuntarily) dragged in at scripted points during the game. It can be described as a more "evil" and more dangerous version of reality, bearing roughly the same structure, but differing heavily in its outward appearance. In the first two games, the normal world turns into a dark, industrial world, "where streets or floors are replaced by rusty grates over bottomless abysses" (Perron, "Sign of a Threat"). The alternate hospital of *SH3* changes even further: While still containing the same industrial elements, the walls in some places glow orange-red, blurring the environment, and with blood and worms covering them, they seem to be alive. This concept is carried to extremes in the chapel, the last level of the game, where blood gradually takes over the complete architecture. Pruett illustrates that the "Otherworld" is usually introduced whenever the developers have increased tension in the "fog" world (the "real" world, the game starts with) and within the Otherworld, "the designers [. . .] slowly crank the pressure on the player up and up and up, until finally, they are released [. . .] and return to the relatively tame Fog World" ("The Changing Utility of the Otherworld in the *Silent Hill* Series").

SH is not gothic anymore, "no castles here", as Niedenthal remarks[63] ("Patterns of Obscurity" 177). At one point, though, *SH3* parodies *RE*'s gothic setting (e.g. the mansion of *RE1* and the clock tower of *RE3*): The amusement park level includes a section named "Borley Haunted Mansion". It consists of four rooms, each hosting a different kind of "spooky" installation, through which the player is guided by a voice coming from a speaker system. The first puts on display a bloody crime scene: a living room, in which a father apparently killed his family. While the player is staring at the scene, power suddenly goes off and lightning visualises the silhouette of a man having been hanged in front of the window. In the second room, a puppet, sitting in a chair is shown from behind, rocking forwards and backwards, that movement being accompanied by a squeaking sound. As soon as players approach the scene in order to trigger another comment, a strapped puppet drops right before

---

[62] For further reference see above (17).

[63] Though Rautzenberg claims *SH*'s fog to stem from gothic horror, as well (134).

them to remain in a headlong position. When examining[64] the "puppet", Heather, the games' protagonist, finds out that it is a real corpse. To players having entered the third room (a prisonlike passage) and having taken a step forward, a low angle reveals the room's spiked ceiling. When the player proceeds further, that ceiling drops only to stop right above the avatar's head[65] (> "HBT"). The last section is a succession of mazelike hallways with folding walls. When the player traverses it, the camera is set in front of the avatar, making navigation difficult. Moreover, an ominous red light follows the avatar, leading to its death by touch. This is a fine example of "trial-and-error"[66], for death will be highly likely for a player who does not know the correct way. He will bump into the walls and die. Although the haunted house is a mere cliché, the calm[67] and subtle mise-en-scène[68] in the rooms works towards the startle effects, they contain.

"Startle effects": Since "Borley Mansion" houses some startle effects, one might be tempted to draw the conclusion that *SH* generally favours them. This is not the case, in fact, it rarely does: *SH1*, for instance, comprises only four scenes, which are of comparable nature, two of them will be described here: The first occurs at the very beginning of the game, when protagonist Harry wakes up in a diner. In an in-game cutscene, a window in the back bursts, Harry, rather distracted, turns around, only to be startled by another bursting window in the front, this time with an actual monster flying through it (> "HBT"). In the elementary school level, the player enters a room full of lockers and hears a hammering sound, implying that something is locked up inside one of them (> "AF"). When it is examined, a cat bolts out. With this incident in mind, the player later confronts a similar situation: Again, a locker needs to be examined. This time, it slowly opens all by itself, revealing nothing but a blood-tainted interior. Relieved, the player steps back, only to be startled by another locker suddenly bursting open and a bloody corpse falling out of it. The startle effects of *SH* work especially well, since they do not appear so often, whereas *RE* tends to overuse them. They are rare, nonetheless, and most of *SH*'s tension stems from other sources, for instance, from its creature design.

---

[64] By pushing a specific button on the controller, nearly every object in the game can be examined by the player. Doing so, a textual comment from the part of the avatar will be the result.

[65] When playing the game in hard mode, the spikes can actually kill the avatar and players need to prevent this by taking a series of specific steps.

[66] Trial-and-error, being a rather unfair method, is generally said to be a negative feature of games (*Gamasutra*). However, survival horror games often bear such negative features (like stiff controls or an uncomfortable saving feature), serving the game's purpose by creating stress (> "ETT").

[67] No music accompanies the events.

[68] "Mise-en-scène", literally translated "to put in scene" (Logas and Muller 1), in the context of games, refers to "convey subtext" (e.g. eliciting emotions) by means of level design.

"Creature design" (> GP): "My basic idea of creating the monsters [. . .] was to give them a human aspect", Masahiro Ito[69] says (*Alchemists of Emotion: The Making of* Silent Hill 2) and with the exception of the "Double Head" dogs (*SH1-3*) and some bosses (e.g. the "Split Worm" in *SH3*), this concept has been consistently applied to the game. Most of *SH*'s denizens are deformed creatures, bearing stronger or lesser similarities to their human inspiration: Whereas the nurses (*SH1-3*) differ from human beings only by their movement[70], the "Mannequins" (*SH2*) have a second pair of legs instead of a torso and the "Slurper" (*SH3*) has a long, funnel-shaped head. The human resemblances are supposed to remind players of themselves, which evokes pity and makes them hesitate to attack the monsters. If it is done, nonetheless, "a last kick is necessary to silence and terminate the abominable creatures", as Perron rightly observes ("Body Genre" 130). When they have been taken down, they remain on the ground, trembling, until we release them. To force the player in such a situation, as Perron goes on, "reminds him that a monstrous Other is hidden inside each of us", since basically, the creatures are helpless, when they lie on the ground. Moreover, this form of "close combat" prevents attacking them from a safe distance: Without the final kick, they will probably get up again and crawl back into the fog or darkness they came from. In turn, they are left with the chance of launching a further attack. This aspect of the game mechanics makes enemies more dangerous and combat closer. The effect is emphasised even more through *SH*'s general preference for melee[71] combat: The first weapon, players in *SH2* obtain, is a wooden board, and large numbers of such weapons (knives, steel pipes etc.) can be picked up throughout the game.

"Darkness and fog" (> GP): For every creator of horror, it seems obvious to take advantage of our primal fears. One of these is the "fear of the dark" which "much classic horror fiction deals with [. . .]" (Rouse, "Match Made in Hell" 19) and *SH*, with its "poor and low acuity lighting" (Niedenthal, "Shadowplay: Simulated Illumination in Game Worlds"), is no exception here. In all games, the player, most of the time, travels through complete darkness, only using a flashlight. On top of that, the area illuminated is very small. Elsewhere, Niedenthal refers to an eyetracking study which led to interesting results regarding our analysis: It revealed that players are constantly scanning the "darkness edge", always expecting monsters to cross it ("Patterns of Obscurity" 178) (> "AF").

---

[69] Ito is one of the game directors of *SH1-3*, as well as their monster designer.

[70] While their heads are twisted, they move along in a stagnant way.

[71] In the context of games, the term "melee weapon" refers to a weapon which is used in hand-to-hand combat.

The same applies to the fog, whose edge was continuously scanned for "an average of 31.5 percent of playing time". Due to the fact that players know that what will step out of the fog will most likely be a monster, it might be argued that they spend one third of their playing time in a state of anticipatory fear (> "AF"). Additionally, both darkness and fog thwart clear perception and provide the monsters with the opportunity to attack from any direction at any time, leading players to detect them rather late. What is more, in the streets, the only places where fog occurs, they can lose their bearings (Rautzenberg 135) and wander around totally disorientated (> "ETT").

"Descent": Another primal fear according to Niedenthal ("Patterns of Obscurity" 175) is "jumping into darkness where one cannot see the bottom of the pit". This and other forms of "descent" are an unsettling experience *SH* occasionally confronts the player with. From the "Historical Society" building (*SH2*), a seemingly endless stairway leads into the darkness. Immediately afterwards, the prison level is entered by jumping into a pitch-black hole on the floor. Dark ducts must be descended (*SH1*, elementary school clock tower) and the rails of a rollercoaster will be walked down (*SH3*, amusement park), while complete darkness surrounds the player. Apart from unsettlement and anxiety a sense of isolation is the result, since players get the feeling of traveling deeper and deeper into the darkness, while they are further and further away from the safe[72] place where they once started (> "ETT").

"Isolation": Isolation in *SH* appears in different forms. At the very beginning of *SH2*, for example, the player needs to walk from a parking lot to the actual town of Silent Hill on foot, crossing a shady forest. While doing that nothing happens and the first enemy is encountered in town, after having walked for about fifteen minutes. The developers had a certain effect in mind, when they provided the game with such a slow start:

> At the beginning of the game, we deliberately made the descent
> through the forest towards the cemetery longer. It's so long you don't
> feel like turning back. At the same time, it makes you realize how totally
> isolated the city is... and you also!
> (*Alchemists of Emotion*)

Kirkland points out that though being "risky in terms of gameplay"[73] ("Discursively Constructing" 324), the sequence is particularly "important in conveying physical and psychological isolation". After having entered town, the roads are blocked by bottomless pits

---

[72] At least *SH2* and *SH3* begin in a rather peaceful environment with no monsters: a deserted parking lot and a mall.

[73] He argues that these long passages might bore certain players.

appearing out of nowhere and the player not only "feels like turning back" (*Alchemists of Emotion*), but simply cannot do it anymore. Thus the mere feeling of isolation, mentioned above, becomes more concrete and visual.

"Fixed Camera": *SH* does not feature pre-rendered backgrounds like *RE*, but real time-animated graphics. Though the camera is typically positioned behind the avatar, developers also pose a fixed camera at certain points (mostly indoors, as in the apartment and the prison level, *SH2*). A most textbook example for an environment "dictated by camera angles" (Kirkland, "Self-Reflexive Funhouse" 412) is the "Haunted Mansion" mentioned above (25-27). When the camera is focusing on something in the foreground and thus confining the avatar to the background (such as in *SH3*'s hospital basement, where the camera is placed on the floor behind a wheelchair), the feeling of being observed is the result (> "ETT"). In contrast, if the camera only focuses on the character and to a minor degree on the room, it "feels like somewhere you could become trapped [. . .] that something could sneak up behind you" as Carr assumes ("Play Dead: Genre and Affect in *Silent Hill* and *Planescape Torment*") (> "AF").

"Subconscious Manipulation": Often, *SH* taps even deeper into the player than usual and facilitates manipulation at the level of their subconscious. Certain visual characteristics of creatures, levels etc. are designed in an ambivalent way, with their meaning being disguised in some way and thus rather working subconsciously. Early in *SH3*, players make the acquaintance of Claudia, the leader of the local cult. The developers created her face without any eyebrows, leaving her expression emotionless and evil. Vincent, another *SH3* NPC ("Non Player Character"), when speaking to players, focuses on them with only one of his eyes, while his other eye stares elsewhere (Silent Hill 3: *Naissance d'une Renaissance*). In the apartment level of *SH2*, the player finds a dead person, sitting in a chair in front of a TV. The developers used the very same model they used for the avatar (*Alchemists of Emotion*). Since the body does not face the player and its identity is further masked because of its blood-stained clothes and skin, there is a slight chance to notice, that it is the player who is sitting dead in that chair. All examples evoke a certain unease on the part of the players, who are induced to feel even more insecure, since they do not know why exactly they are frightened (> "ETT").

"Blood and gore" (> AUD): *SH*'s horror is not always psychological in the way discussed in the previous paragraph. Sometimes, the "cheap scare" of blood and gore makes its appearance. During the mall level of *SH3*, a cutscene shows the giant "Closer" creature, chewing on the head of a corpse, lying on the floor. Some rooms later, a special key needs to be retrieved from the gashed stomach of a grilled dog, which is served on a tray. Mangled corpses in crucified positions hang in one of the toilets of the elementary school and in the boat, where it is stuck to its bulkhead (*SH1*). As in *RE*, disgust is most likely triggered by observing such imagery (> "ETT").

"Cutscenes" (> AUD, NARR): Just like *RE*, *SH* includes both in-game and CGI cutscenes. Whereas in *RE* the former are the preferred vehicle for creating tension, *SH* uses both for that purpose. In the subway level of *SH3*, an in-game cutscene is triggered, when the player is approaching the rails. Heather is shown through the eyes of someone (or something), who (or which) is approaching her, breathing stertorously, and finally pushing her onto the tracks. After getting up again, there is no sign of any presence and there will not be for the rest of the game. By leaving players in such uncertainty and giving them no opportunity to fight their invisible enemy, it is likely that they will feel threatened for a longer period in anticipation of a further attack (> "AF"). When entering the hospital roof in *SH2*, a suddenly triggered cutscene shows "Pyramid Head"[74], violently pushing the player against a fence, which then caves in, with the player falling down into the darkness. A room in *SH3*'s hospital contains a locker with a telephone inside, which starts ringing. In case the player answers the call, an obscure dialogue will be triggered: "[. . .] Happy birthday to you, happy birthday to you, happy birthday, dear... oh, I forgot your name! [. . .]" (*Silent Hill 3*). The recorded voice speaks in an unsettling and violently accentuated manner, making the ordinarily harmless content sound threatening. Another phone call is taken in the otherworld counterpart of the elementary school (*SH1*), with the protagonist's missing daughter[75] crying for help at the end of the line. These two cutscenes provide an uncanny effect, since it is unsettling to hear a familiar sound indicating presence and liveliness in an environment which stands for the exact opposite: desolation and death. This concept is picked up again in the amusement park level (*SH3*). Turning a usually happy place into one of horror is, according to Kirschke,

---

[74] This monster is occasionally encountered in *SH2*, similar to "Nemesis" in *RE3*. In contrast to "Nemesis", however, "Pyramid Head" is fought against only once, at the end of the game. Before that, he appears with the mere intention to scare us.

[75] The game starts with a car crash, in which Cheryl, the daughter of protagonist Harry, vanishes. Since the player's main goal during the game is to retrieve her, worry might be felt resulting from the call (>"ETT").

considerably more unsettling than using a setting being so anyway[76] (qtd. in Klatt, "Augen Zu und durch" 68).

Examples for tension resulting from CGI cutscenes are taken from *SH1*: In the hospital, Harry frequently meets a nurse named Lisa. Later, the player gets to know that in reality she is dead and just a kind of ghost, which is still wandering around. To underline that, she starts bleeding from her forehead, so that her face is completely covered with blood. The ending of *SH1* includes a cutscene in which the character Dr. Kaufmann is dragged into the darkness by the very same Lisa. His fate remains uncertain for us.

"Irritation": Often, the conventions of game design are subverted to put players into situations they have never been confronted with before. One of the toilets in *SH1*'s elementary school is a sort of elevator which leads to the second floor. However, neither any movement nor sound indicates that players have traveled there. They enter and leave the room to find themselves in a completely different location. The last level, called "Nowhere", is a series of locations, which the player has already visited before. They are attached to one another in a way that disturbs "the spacial coherence and cause-and-effect logic which determines adventure game structure" (Kirkland, "Self-Reflexive Funhouse" 407). Moreover, no map is available, turning this section into a maze the player easily gets lost in. Sometimes, game components just appear out of nowhere, like a fourth elevator button in a building with three floors (*SH1*, hospital) or a door at the end of a hallway (*SH3*, hospital). These techniques are likely to create confusion, helplessness or even panic, when the player gets lost in the "labyrinthine space" of *SH2*'s prison maze and keeps running into "Pyramid Head" (Niedenthal, "Patterns of Obscurity" 175) (> "ETT").

4.2.2 Gameplay Techniques

"Warning systems" (> AUD, VIS): An essential part of *SH*'s gameplay is the simultaneous use of radio and flashlight. Both have the function of a "warning system", a device signaling the presence of monsters (Perron, "Sign of a Threat"). The radio does that through the emission of a static noise, while the flashlight simply helps the player to detect monsters in the dark. Paradoxically, both are equally helpful as they are responsible for some of our anxiety. On the one hand, when switched on, light and/or sound attract the monsters' attention, making exploration a more dangerous endeavour. On the other hand, the warning sound of the radio also increases the anticipatory fear, since it constantly reminds us of the monsters' presence (> "AF"). A normally reliable warning device, the radio does not work in

---

[76] Such as the morgue in *RE2*.

the sewers (*SH1*). Players are not informed about that and since the radio remains silent, they might conclude that there is no threat at all. Unexpectedly being confronted with a new monster, a frog-like creature which can drop from the ceiling, will terrify them.

"Respawning enemies": In some of the levels of *SH1* and *SH3*, especially the mall and the hospital, enemies tend to respawn, meaning that they have previously been defeated, but show up again at the same place. While this is a common thing in other game genres (most notably action games), it is not in survival horror and since it happens irregulary, it is also not predictable.

"Weak avatar" (> AUD, VIS): Although *RE* also has "weak avatars", they are made weak merely externally through the application of certain game mechanics as discussed in our definition of survival horror: by e.g. limiting health and ammunition supplies. The avatars themselves remain professionally trained mercenaries. Those of *SH*, on the contrary, are altogether everymen with no special abilities and the games visualise their weaknesses: When they are in a state of near death (and when they run for longer periods), they are heavily breathing and leaning forwards. This is emphasised by the game mechanics, since most attacks are carried out with the help of melee weapons[77]. "Using a frail-looking character [. . .] enables designers to achieve scares with less effort", as Pruett argues ("Designing Characters"). He continues by pointing out that this is so because it is easier to "identify with the characters, who are in dangerous situations". When the characters are as weak as players are (and the typical player is most probably not a mercenary), certain emotions such as worry (Ekman and Lankoski 197) can be provoked more easily (> "ETT").

4.2.3 Audio Techniques

"General sound and music score": *SH* sound designer Akira Yamaoka describes *RE*'s sounds as "pretty formal", that "we are pretty used to hearing them" (*Alchemists of Emotion*). He refers to the fact that its sounds are similar to their real-life counterparts, meaning a footstep sounds like a footstep and a gunshot like a gunshot. In regard to *SH2*, he further states, it was "tried to create something that would surprise you [. . .], something that would challenge your imagination". For this reason, the sources of the recorded sounds are less obvious: The grunt of the "Closer" creature, for instance, is that of a rhinoceros. Music either bears an "industrial style", with the creators "incorporating mechanical sounds as part of the music" (Whalen), or it consists of calmer acoustic guitar, ambient and drum and bass music. The industrial sound accompanies action sequences (like fighting monsters, mostly in the "Otherworld"), whereas

---

[77] For further reference see above (28).

the acoustic guitar usually underscores cutscenes. In the "Fog" world, music is completely missing, which makes the following "Otherworld"-sequences more effective (> "ETT"). In *RE*, music accompanies almost every level and scene, whereas in *SH*, to quote Yamaoka again, "silence is also a sound".

"Off-screen sounds": On the one hand, the off-screen sounds of *RE*[78] are employed in the same way and with the same effect in *SH:* The player generally hears (and fears) the monsters before he sees them, for instance, the "Numb Body" with its donkey-like bray in *SH3*'s mall (> "AF"). On the other hand, acousmatic sound effects find a rather different and more original use. On some occasions, the sound of footsteps (which are not the players') can be heard. While walking through the woods of *SH2*[79], players perceive them as originating from the coppice next to them. "If the player stops, the sounds instantly go silent" (Ekman and Lankoski 194), implying that someone is following the player. In *SH3*'s office building level, someone seems to walk around one floor above us. This effect works particularly well, if the player is equipped with a surround system, because the sounds seem to move across the room. More footsteps are heard in the amusement park fortune house and the church (*SH3*). Although their sound also implies the presence of someone or something, we cannot see but only hear, they present a contrast to the off-screen sound of approaching enemies, whose identity is at least known to us. These "suggestive and worrisome noises" (Carr, "Play Dead") also contribute to the "psychological" horror of *SH*.

4.2.4 Narrative Techniques

"Moral decisions": By evoking pity through creature design[80] the developers practise a technique which makes the players feel unsettled and tests their morale[81]. On some occasions, *SH* exposes them to similar situations: *SH3*'s chapel level contains a confession booth, in which the player, in the role of the confessor, has the choice between absolving or not absolving the anonymous person on the other side. According to the developers themselves, whatever the player opts for will be wrong (*Naissance d'une Renaissance*). Nevertheless, players have to make a decision either way and the inevitability of this places them into a highly unpleasant situation. The boss fight against the possessed Cybil, an otherwise friendly NPC (*SH1*), can be "won" by either killing her or using a certain key item to exorcise the

---

[78] For further reference see above (24).
[79] For further reference see above (29).
[80] For further reference see above (28).
[81] Especially in modern role playing games, this has become a trend. Both the *Mass Effect* (Microsoft/Bioware, 2007-10) and modern *Fallout* titles (Bethesda, 2008-10), comprise moral decision taking as part of their gameplay, since it makes the characters and the relationships between them appear more realistic.

demon inside her. The latter is rather difficult to accomplish, however, since the key item has not necessarily been collected. Thus killing her is the more likely outcome and certain players might feel guilty after having done so (> "ETT"). Guilt is also triggered in *SH3*, though in a cutscene: When Heather refers to the monsters, which she has killed, Vincent replies: "Monsters? They looked like monsters to you?" (*Silent Hill 3*). This implies that Heather may only be hallucinating and has in fact killed other beings than monsters (i.e. humans).

"Explicit scenes" (> VIS, AUD): For a start, this category is not to be confused with "blood and gore". By "explicit", rather disturbing content other than that is referred to. Such an example can be found in *SH2*, for example: "Pyramid Head" is encountered for the first time in the apartment level at the beginning of the game. He is shown raping another enemy character, which is watched by the protagonist, who is hidden in the wardrobe[82]. Alexander reckons this scene to be "one of the most disturbing scenes in video game history" ("Sundering the Mind"). Another socio-cultural taboo is broken at the end of *SH3*: In a cutscene, Heather performs an "oral abortion" by regurgitating an embryo. Even more delicate is the fact, that this embryo is supposed to be "God", as stated by the game's narrative.

"No Happy Ending": The *SH* universe rarely offers the player a typical happy ending. Most games disssolve in an unsatisfactory and blurred way or feature a depressing twist in their plot. *SH1*'s "bad ending"[83] leaves the player with the protagonist (and virtually all other characters) being dead and his daughter vanished. *SH2* ends with the revelation that the protagonist has killed his wife, because he could not bear her severe illness any longer. At the end of *SH3*, we have to kill "God"[84]. In comparison, all *RE*-games come to a true Hollywood-style conclusion, with a nuclear explosion and the protagonists escaping by helicopter (*RE1/RE2*) or by train (*RE2*). Possible negative emotions triggered by this, technically cannot produce tension anymore (since the games end with them), but we turn off our consoles with a bad feeling, taking the horror along with us.

---

[82] A part of this sequence, when James is shown from the side looking through a slot in the wardrobe's door, is inspired by an almost identical scene in David Lynch's film *Blue Velvet* (1986).

[83] All games have various endings, depending on certain actions of the player. If players manage to collect the "Flauros" key item, for example, and use it on the roof of the lighthouse, they are rewarded with the secret "U.F.O."-ending. These multiple endings are typical of survival horror games.

[84] Though "God" is embodied by a horrific monster.

4.2.5 Miscellaneous Techniques

"Vibration": The vibrational function of the controller is used similar to the way it is used in *RE* by emphasizing certain types of collisions, enemy confrontations, sounds etc. Additionally, it is used "to make visible (or rather, tactile) some physical features of a player character" (Lankoski 5). In *SH1* the controller vibrates whenever the avatar's health is low, simulating and accompanying its heartbeat (accelerating the more health is lost). This makes it another "warning system" next to radio and flashlight and produces stress and panic, for players know that they are in danger and need to restore their health as quickly as possible (> "AF"/"ETT").

5 Conclusion

This paper has sought to find out how the survival horror game series *Resident Evil* and *Silent Hill* manage to elicit tension and other emotions, as suggested by the "Excitation-Transfer Theory". In order to provide respective evidence, the author of this paper has not only tried to identify as many of the "scare techniques", deployed by developers as possible, but also to juxtapose them in order to point out their differences. The results will be referred to and presented in this final account, which incidentally also attempts to assess the effectiveness of these techniques (as well as the series).

To begin with, since all games belong to the same genre (i.e. survival horror), they share some of their main characteristics, notably those which are connected to producing tension: their limited resources in conjunction with the large number of enemies (laid down by the game mechanics and the ruleset) cause stress and anxiety, whereas enclosed spaces and narrow hallways (provided by the environment) ought to evoke a claustrophobic effect. Other than that, the "startle effects" provoking shock are included in both their repertories, the same is true for the "uncanny" settings, cutscenes, creature and sound design, to give but a few prominent examples. Therefore, with a few exceptions, such as *Resident Evil*'s invulnerable enemies and time limits, or *Silent Hill*'s use of fog/darkness and warning systems, both series generally utilise the same techniques. Taking a closer look at these techniques individually, however, reveals that most of them vary greatly: environments are prototypically gothic horror in *Resident Evil*, *Silent Hill* breaks away from that pattern as soon as the twisted "Otherworld" appears. The same applies to the music, which, again, draws on traditional horror films in *Resident Evil*, whereas *Silent Hill* technically uses a cacophony of various sound effects rather than music to create a certain effect. The same tendency is reflected in creature design: *Resident Evil* contains zombies, spiders and all sorts of mutants, *Silent Hill* takes a unique approach by introducing disfigured monsters, inspired by Bacon and Bosch (Perron, "Body Genre" 128; *Alchemists of Emotion*).

Turning towards the difficult aspect of the efficiency of scare techniques, it must be repeated once more that feeling an emotion remains a subjective activity. In order to make progress, subjectivity is to be left out of account, so that theories may be focused on instead: "Hitchcock's Bomb Theory" has taught us that tension is supposed to be a more powerful emotion than shock. Shock, as has been found out, mostly comes in the form of startle effects in a survival horror game. *Resident Evil* contains a considerably higher amount of startle effects, whereas *Silent Hill* gets along with very few of them and, in addition, deploys them more cautiously. Thus there is a longer interval between them, meaning "longer anticipation" according to the Schachter and Singer experiment. This makes them probably more effective in *Silent Hill*. But yet, anticipatory fear, as has been found out, is involved in many of the techniques of both games, not only in their startle effects: *Resident Evil*'s fixed camera (and *Silent Hill*'s darkness and fog) has been said to create anticipatory fear, as well. Hence, it could also be inferred that, since the fixed camera is omnipresent in *Resident Evil*, the same applies to anticipatory fear and tension.

It comes as no surprise then that it is almost impossible to assess a certain degree of "terrifying quality" in our games. Yet, a last humble try will be made, by drawing on the "fundamental style" of the two series, which means that they will be looked at as a whole. *Silent Hill* has commonly been thought of as "psychological horror" (e.g., by Picard 111), whose essence is "the unknown" (Wolfsteiner 169) and "the unseen" (Roux-Girard 145). Apart from the fixed camera, hiding the monsters, *Resident Evil* leaves not much to the player's imagination, whereas *Silent Hill*'s horror is mainly implicit. This may be illustrated by a very simple example: Dead bodies can frequently be found in the levels of both series as a "decoration". While in *Resident Evil 1*, a certain body is clearly identified as "the body of Forest" ("He's been picked to death by crows!", *Resident Evil*), the same is merely implied in *Silent Hill* by "something" being hidden under a blanket (rather than someone specific being depicted) and Rouse recalls that "horror works best the less that is explained" ("Match Made in Hell" 16). Generally, the series scares players in such subtle ways, for example by subconsciously manipulating them through hidden symbolism, appealing to our primal fears, or even by fundamentally shattering our moral convictions. Apart from that, it uses rather drastic techniques, like the often cacophonous sound design or distressing visuals (such as the bleeding and glaring walls in *Silent Hill 3*). "Distressing" as it often is, *Silent Hill*, with its "more imaginative and subtle anticipatory dread" is rather survival "terror" than "horror", as Perron rightly observes, being in stark contrast to *Resident Evil*, with its "perceptible, comprehensible, measurable [. . .] material" ("Sign of a Threat").

Suggestions for further Research

As a coda, it has to be pointed out that the above analysis is definitely far from exhaustive. Ascertaining a holistic "fear system" of survival horror games will require further work by researchers, as it has been found very little data in this paper. Many other techniques triggering tension in a survival horror game could be analysed, which have been discussed either rudimentarily or not at all in this paper: little has been said about tension resulting from the plot, for instance, and even less about altering the pace of a game (i.e. changing the game tone). Especially the former is considered to be an important aspect in creating tension (e.g., by Niedenthal, "Patterns of Obscurity" 174).

Works Cited

Aarseth, Espen. *Cybertext: Perspectives on Ergodic Literature*. Baltimore and London: John Hopkins UP, 1997. Print.

Alchemists of Emotion: The Making of Silent Hill 2. Dir. Nicolas Beuglet. Fun TV, 2001. DVD.

Alexander, Leigh. "Sundering the Mind." *The Aberrant Gamer Column*. Game Set Watch, 19 July 2007. Web. 25 June 2011. <http://www.gamesetwatch.com/2007/07/the _aberrant_ gamer_sundering_the_mind.php>.

"Anime." *Macmillan's English Dictionary for Advanced Learners*. 2002. Print.

Barraza, Clara. "Memories, like the Blood-Stained Colours of My Mind: The Evolution of the Survival Horror Genre." *IGN.com* (2008). Web. 25 June 2011. <http://uk.pc.ign.com/articles/906/906852p1.html>.

Beech, Alex. "Are Horror Games Becoming Less Scary?" *Videogame Reviews.co.uk*. VGR Network, 23 Sep. 2009. Web. 25 June 2011. <http://www.videogame-reviews.co.uk/index.php?s=are+horror+games+becoming+less+scary>.

Blum, Benjamin. "Resident Evil." *GamePro* Mar. 2009: 26-27. Print.

Bopp, Matthias, Neitzel, Britta, and Rolf F. Nohr. Introduction. *See? I'm Real: Multidisziplinäre Zugänge zum Computerspiel am Beispiel von* Silent Hill. By Neitzel, Bopp, and Nohr, eds. Münster: Lit, 2004: 7-13.

Buecheler, Christopher. "Hall of Fame: *Haunted House*." *Gamespy.com*. IGN Entertainment, 8 Dec. 2002. Web. 25 June 2011. <http://www.gamespy.com/articles/ 490/490366p1.html>.

Bustami, H. P. "Arachnophobia: Why Spiders Are Disgusting." Life of Science. 2 Dec. 2008. Web. 25 June 2011. <http://www.life-of-science.net/zoology-and-botany/feature /arachnophobia---why-spiders-are-disgusting.html>.

Capcom, dev. *Resident Evil*. n.p. Capcom, 1996. Computer Game.

---. *Resident Evil 2*. n.p. Capcom, 1998. Computer Game.

---. *Resident Evil 3: Nemesis*. n.p. Capcom, 1999. Computer Game.

Carr, Diane. "Play Dead: Genre and Affect in *Silent Hill* and *Planescape Torment*." *Game Studies: The International Journal of Computer Game Research* 3.1 (2003): n. pag. Web. 25 June 2011. <http://www.gamestudies.org/0301/carr/>.

---. "Textual Analysis, Digital Games, Zombies." *DiGRA: The Digital Games Research Association* (2009): 1-8. Web. 25 June 2011. <http://www.digra.org/dl/db/09287.24171.pdf>.

Cheng, Paul. "Waiting For Something to Happen: Narratives, Interactivity and Agency and the Videogame Cut-Scene." *DiGRA: The Digital Games Research Association* (2007): 15-24. Web. 25 June 2011. <http://www.digra.org/dl/db/07311.24415.pdf>.

"Cut-Scene." *Half-Real: A Dictionary of Videogame Theory*. Jesper Juul. Web. 25 June 2011. <http://www.half-real.net/dictionary/>.

Degler, Frank. "Erspielte Geschichten: Labyrinthisches Erzählen im Computerspiel." Neitzel, Bopp and Nohr 58-73.

Dymek, Mikolaj. "Exporting Wars: Literature Theory and How It Explains the Video Game Industry." *DiGRA: The Digital Games Research Association* (2007): 664-71. Web. 25 June 2011. <http://www.digra.org/dl/db/07311.32393.pdf>.

Ekman, Inger, and Petri Lankoski. "Hair-Rising Entertainment: Emotions, Sound, and Structure in *Silent Hill 2* and *Fatal Frame*." Perron 181-99.

Ernst, Henry. "Mein gruseligstes Videospiel-Erlebnis." *GamePro* Mar. 2009: 24-25. Print.

Eskelinen, Markku. "The Gaming Situation." *Game Studies: The International Journal of Computer Game Research* 1.1 (2001): n. pag. Web. 25 June 2011. <http://www.gamestudies.org/0101/eskelinen/>.

Evans-Thirlwell, Edwin. "Putting the Horror Back in Survival Horror: The *Silent Hill Shattered Memories* Team Talk Genre Reinvention." *Videogames Daily.com*. Kikizo Network, 12 Feb. 2010. Web. 25 June 2011. <http://videogamesdaily.com/interviews/201002/putting-the-horror-back-in-survival-horror/>.

"Fear." Def. 1. *Macmillan's English Dictionary for Advanced Learners*. 2002. Print.

Fesler, Mario. *Archive der Angst: Räume und Raumgestaltung in den Videospielen Resident Evil 3 Nemesis und Silent Hill*. München [Munich] and Ravensburg: Grin Verlag für akademische Texte, 2007. Print.

Forster, Winnie. *Computer- und Videospiel-Macher.* Utting: Gameplan, 2008. Print.

Gamasutra. ABM Techweb. Web. 25 June 2011. <http://www.gamasutra.com/blogs
/ThomasGrip/20100412/4905/Why_Trial_and_Error_will_Doom_Games.php>.

Giantbomb. Whiskey Media. Web. 25 June 2011. <http://www.giantbomb.com/>.

Hoeger, Laura, and William Huber. "Ghastly Multiplication: *Fatal Frame II* and the
Videogame Uncanny." *DiGRA: The Digital Games Research Association* (2007):
152-56. Web. 25 June 2011. <http://www.digra.org/dl/db/07313.12302.pdf>.

Järvinen, Aki. *Games Without Frontiers: Theories and Methods for Game Studies and
Design.* Diss. U of Tampere, 2008. Saarbrücken: VDM Verlag, 2009. Print.

Juul, Jesper. *Half-Real: Video Games between Real Rules and Fictional Worlds.* Cambridge:
MIT Press, 2005. Print.

King, Geoff, and Tanya Krzywinska. "Computer Games/Cinema/Interfaces." *DiGRA: The
Digital Games Research Association* (2002): 141-53. Web. 25 June 2011.
<http://www.digra.org/dl/db/05164.41114.pdf>.

Kirkland, Ewan. "Discursively Constructing the Art of *Silent Hill.*" *Games and Culture* 5
(2010): 314-28. Web. 25 June 2011. <http://gac.sagepub.com/content/5/3/314
.full.pdf+html>.

---. "Horror Videogames and the Uncanny." *DiGRA: The Digital Games Research
Association* (2009): 1-4. Web. 25 June 2011.
<http://www.digra.org/dl/db/09287.25453.pdf>.

---. "Maternal Engulfment in Horror Videogames." *Video Games Cultures and
Future Interactive Entertainment* (2010): 1-7. Web. 25 June 2011. <http://www.inter-
disciplinary.net/wp-content/uploads/2009/06/Kirkland-paper.pdf>.

---. "*Resident Evil*'s Typewriter: Survival Horror and Its Remediations." *Games and
Culture* 4 (2008): 115-26. Web. 25 June 2011.
<http://gac.sagepub.com/content/4/2/115>.

---. "The Self-Reflexive Funhouse of *Silent Hill.*" *Convergence: The International
Journal of Research into New Media Technologies* 13 (2007): 403-15. Web. 25 June
2011. <http://con.sagepub.com/content/13/4/403.full.pdf+html>.

---. "Storytelling in Survival Horror Videogames." Perron 62-78.

Klatt, Oliver. "Augen zu und durch." *GEE: Love for Games* June 2007: 66-68. Print.

---. "Im Herzen der Finsternis." *GEE: Love for Games* Apr. 2008: 70-74. Print.

Konami, dev. *Silent Hill*. n.p. Konami, 1999. Computer Game.

---. *Silent Hill 2*. n.p. Konami, 2001. Computer Game.

---. *Silent Hill 3*. n.p. Konami, 2003. Computer Game.

Kringiel, Danny. "Wer das liest, ist nicht doof.". *GEE: Love for Games* 18, 2006: 16. Print.

Krzywinska, Tanya. "Reanimating Lovecraft: The Ludic Paradox of *Call of Cthulhu: Dark Corners of the Earth*." Perron 267-87.

Lange, Andreas. "*Silent Hill 2*: Eine Einführung." Neitzel, Bopp and Nohr 15-19.

Lankoski, Petri. "Building and Reconstructing Character: A Case Study of *Silent Hill 3*." *DiGRA: The Digital Games Research Association* (2005): 1-7. Web. 25 June 2011. <http://www.digra.org/dl/db/06278.03293.pdf>.

Lay, Samantha. "Audiences across the Divide: Game to Film Adaptation and the Case of *Resident Evil*." *Participations: Journal of Audience and Reception Studies* 4 (2009): 1-43. Web. 25 June 2011. <http://www.participations.org/Volume%204/Issue %202/4_02_lay.htm>.

LeDoux, Joseph. *The Emotional Brain: The Mysterious Underpinnings of Emotional Life*. New York: Simon and Schuster, 1996. Print.

Lee, Kwan Min, and Wie Peng. "What Do We Know about Social and Psychological Effects of Computer Games? A Comprehensive Review of the Current Literature." Vorderer, Peter, and Jennings Bryant, eds. *Playing Video Games: Motives, Responses and Consequences*. Philadelphia: Lawrence Erlbaum Assoc. Inc., 2006. Print.

Logas, Heather, and Daniel Muller. "Mise-En-Scène Applied to Level Design: Adapting a Holistic Approach to Level Design." *DiGRA: The Digital Games Research Association* (2005): 1-8. Web. 25 June 2011. <http://www.digra.org/dl/db/ 06276.13262.pdf>.

McCrea, Christian. "Gaming's Hauntology: Dead Media in *Dead Rising*, *Siren* and *Michigan: Report from Hell*." Perron 220-37.

McRoy, Jay. "The Horror Is Alive: Immersion, Spectatorship, and the Cinematics of Fear in the Survival Horror Genre." *Reconstruction* 6.1 (2006): n. pag. Web. 25 June 2011. <http://reconstruction.eserver.org/061/mcroy.shtml>.

Metacritic. CBS Interactive. Web. 25 June 2011. <http://www.metacritic.com/game/xbox-360/dead-space-2>.

Moby Games. Gamefly Media. Web. 25 June 2011. <http://www.mobygames.com/>.

Neitzel, Britta, Matthias Bopp, and Rolf F. Nohr, eds. *See? I'm Real: Multidisziplinäre Zugänge zum Computerspiel am Beispiel von Silent Hill.* Münster: Lit, 2004. Print.

Neitzel, Britta. "Wer bin ich? Thesen zur Avatar-Spieler-Bindung." Neitzel, Bopp and Nohr 193-212.

Niedenthal, Simon. "Patterns of Obscurity: Gothic Setting and Light in *Resident Evil 4* and *Silent Hill 2.*" Perron 168-80.

---. "Shadowplay: Simulated Illumination in Game Worlds." *DiGRA: The Digital Games Research Association* (2005): n. pag. Web. 25 June 2011. <http://www.digra.org/dl/db/06276.16497.pdf>.

Perron, Bernard, comp. and ed. *Horror Video Games: Essays on the Fusion of Fear and Play.* Jefferson: Mcfarland and Co Inc., 2009. Print.

Perron, Bernard. "Gaming after Dark." Introduction. *Horror Video Games: Essays on the Fusion of Fear and Play.* By Perron, ed. Jefferson: Mcfarland and Co Inc., 2009: 3-13.

---. "Sign of a Threat: The Effects of Warning Systems in Survival Horror Games" *Cosign Proceedings* (2004): n. pag. Web. 25 June 2011 <http://ludicine.ca/sites/ludicine.ca/files/Perron_Cosign_2004.pdf>.

---. "The Survival Horror: The Extended Body Genre." Perron 121-43.

Picard, Martin. "Haunting Backgrounds: Transnationality and Intermediality in Japanese Survival Horror Video Games." Perron 95-120.

Pinchbeck, Dan. "Shock, Horror: First-Person Gaming, Horror, and the Art of Ludic Manipulation." Perron 79-94.

Pruett, Chris. "Designing Characters to Be Scared For." *Chris' Survival Horror Quest*. Chris Pruett, 2005. Web. 25 June 2011. <http://www.dreamdawn.com/sh/features /character_design.php>.

---. "Ingredients of Horror: More about the Two-Factor Theory of Emotion." *Chris' Survival Horror Quest*. Chris Pruett, 2010. Web. 25 June 2011. <http://www.dreamdawn.com/sh/post_view.php?index=7977>.

---. "Ingredients of Horror: Two-Factor and Horror Game Design." *Chris' Survival Horror Quest*. Chris Pruett, 2011. Web. 25 June 2011. <http://www.dreamdawn.com /sh/post_view.php?index=7979>.

---. "Resident Evil 4." *Chris' Survival Horror Quest*. Chris Pruett, n.d. Web. 25 June 2011. <http://www.dreamdawn.com/sh/info.php?name=Resident+Evil+4% 2C+Biohazard+4>.

---. "Silent Hill 4." *Chris' Survival Horror Quest*. Chris Pruett, n.d. Web. 25 June 2011. <http://www.dreamdawn.com/sh/info.php?name=Silent+Hill+4%2C +Silent+Hill+4%3A+The+Room>.

---. "The Changing Utility of the Otherworld in the *Silent Hill* Series." *Chris' Survival Horror Quest*. Chris Pruett, 2007. Web. 25 June 2011. <http://www.dreamdawn.com/sh/features/otherworld.php>.

Rautzenberg, Markus. "Vom Rauschen des Realen: Zur Geburt des Unheimlichen aus dem Geist des Mediums in *Silent Hill 2*." Neitzel, Bopp and Nohr 126-44.

Rouse, Richard III. "Games on the Verge of a Nervous Breakdown: Emotional Content in Computer Games." *Computer Graphics* 35.1 (2001): 6-10. Web. 25 June 2011. <http://portal.acm.org/citation.cfm?id=377032&retn=1>.

---. "Match Made in Hell: The Inevitable Success of the Horror Genre in Video Games." Perron 15-25.

Roux-Girard, Guillaume. "Plunged Alone into Darkness: Evolution in the Staging of Fear in the *Alone in the Dark* Series." Perron 145-67.

Schmidt, Kai, and Henry Ernst. "GamePro-Dossier: *Resident Evil*." *GamePro* Sep. 2006: 77-92. Print.

Schumacher, Carsten, and Christian Steinbrink. "Postrock: Nenn mich nicht so." *Intro* Mar. 2011: 121-29. Print.

Sterling, Jim. "Fear 101: A Beginner's Guide to Survival Horror." *IGN.com*. IGN Entertainment, 9 June 2008. Web. 25 June 2011. <http://uk.retro.ign.com /articles/880/880202p1.html>.

Silent Hill 3: *Naissance d'une Renaissance*. Dir. Nicolas Beuglet. We Productions, 2003. DVD.

Tamborini, Ron, James Stiff, and Carl Heidel. "Reacting to Graphic Horror: A Model of Empathy and Emotional Behaviour." *Communication Research* 17 (1990): 616-40. Web. 25 June 2011. <http://crx.sagepub.com/content/17/5/616.full.pdf+html>.

Taylor, Laurie N. "Gothic Bloodlines in Survival Horror Gaming." Perron 46-61.

"Tension." Def. 1a. *Macmillan's English Dictionary for Advanced Learners*. 2002. Print.

Therrien, Carl. "Games of Fear: A Multi-Faceted Historical Account of the Horror Genre in Video Games." Perron 26-45.

Todd, Brett. "Ghouls, Ghosts and Long-Legged Beasts: A Modern History of Horror Games, Part 1." *GameSpot.com*. CBS Interactive, 2009. Web. 12 Apr. 2011. <http://uk.gamespot.com/gamespot/features/pc/history_horror_pt1/p2_01.html>.

Walz, Steffen P. "Extreme Game Design: Spielrhetorische Überlegungen zur Methodik des Grauens." Neitzel, Bopp and Nohr 145-56.

Weise, Matthew. "The Rules of Horror: Procedural Adaptation in *Clock Tower, Resident Evil* and *Dead Rising*." Perron 238-66.

Whalen, Zach. "Play Along: An Approach to Videogame Music." *Game Studies: The International Journal of Computer Game Research* 4.1 (2004): n. pag. Web. 25 June 2011. <http://www.gamestudies.org/0401/whalen/>.

Wiemer, Serjoscha. "Horror, Ekel und Affekt: *Silent Hill 2* als somatisches Erlebnisangebot." Neitzel, Bopp and Nohr 177-92.

Wolfsteiner, Andreas. "Einige Bemerkungen zu Suche und Angst im digitalen Problemraum *Silent Hill 2*." Neitzel, Bopp and Nohr 157-76.

Lightning Source UK Ltd.
Milton Keynes UK
UKOW05f2111171013

219280UK00001B/152/P